KV-697-851

your finances

withdrawn

9030 00000 4124 1

EXPRESS NEWSPAPERS

non-retirement guides

your finances

A practical guide to tax, investments, IFAs and wills

Edited by Frances Kay

KOGAN PAGE

Publisher's note

Every possible effort has been made to ensure that the information contained in this book is accurate at the time of going to press, and the publishers and the author cannot accept responsibility for any errors or omissions, however caused. No responsibility for loss or damage occasioned to any person acting, or refraining from action, as a result of the material in this publication can be accepted by the editor, the publisher or the author.

First published in Great Britain in 2009 by Kogan Page Limited

Apart from any fair dealing for the purposes of research or private study, or criticism or review, as permitted under the Copyright, Designs and Patents Act 1988, this publication may only be reproduced, stored or transmitted, in any form or by any means, with the prior permission in writing of the publishers, or in the case of reprographic reproduction in accordance with the terms and licences issued by the CLA. Enquiries concerning reproduction outside these terms should be sent to the publishers at the undermentioned address:

Kogan Page Limited
120 Pentonville Road
London N1 9JN
United Kingdom
www.koganpage.com

© Kogan Page, 2009

The right of Kogan Page to be identified as the author of this work has been asserted by them in accordance with the Copyright, Designs and Patents Act 1988.

British Library Cataloguing in Publication Data

A CIP record for this book is available from the British Library.

ISBN 978 0 7494 5584 2

Typeset by Jean Cussons Typesetting, Diss, Norfolk
Printed and bound in Great Britain by MPG Books Ltd, Bodmin, Cornwall

LONDON BOROUGH OF WANDSWORTH	
9030 00000 4124 1	
Askews	09-Jul-2009
332.024 KAY	£5.99
	WWX0005038/0044

Contents

Introduction

While you're working you don't have much time to think about retirement. But planning ahead is common sense. In retirement your money should be made to go as far as possible because living on a fixed (or as is sometimes the case a shrinking) income requires forethought. Making the most of what you've got is sensible and advisable; this is what will be dealt with in the following pages. Working out how much tax you will pay, or can save, is the first thing. Assessing your likely savings, including lump sums from your pension or any insurance policies you may have can give you a much clearer idea of the future. From this you can draw up a plan as to how to maximise their value. The advice is offered as a prompt because each person's situation is unique. You may need to consider whether you should invest your money in a building society, ISA, unit trust, stocks and shares or government securities. Would it make sense to buy an annuity? What tax planning should you consider in your position? It is always wise to consult a good accountant, stockbroker or other professional adviser. If you do not have one there is advice on how to find the right person. With a bit of time spent wisely now, you should reap the benefits for many years to come.

1

Tax

As everyone knows, there are two certainties – death and taxes. So a book that gives information on taxes, as well as how to invest what money you have, is appropriate. Although over the years you may have been contributing many thousands of pounds to the Inland Revenue (now called **HM Revenue & Customs** or **HMRC**, for short), in practice you may have had very little direct contact with the tax system. The accounts department will have automatically deducted – and accounted for – the PAYE on your earnings as a salaried employee. If you were self-employed or had other money unconnected with your job, you may have had more dealings with your tax office.

Come retirement, even though for most people the issues are not particularly complex, a little basic knowledge can be invaluable. First, it will help you to calculate how much money (after deduction of tax) you will have available to spend: the equivalent, if you like, of your take-home pay. At a more sophisticated level, understanding the broad principles could help you save money by not paying more in taxation than you need.

Income tax

This is calculated on all (or nearly all) your income, after deduction of your personal allowance; and, in the case of older married people, of the married couple's allowance. The reason for saying 'nearly all' is that some income you may receive is tax-free: types of income on which you do not have to pay tax are listed a little further on.

Most income counts, however. You will be assessed for income tax on: your pension, interest you receive from most types of savings, dividends from investments, any earnings (even if these are only from casual work), plus rent from any lodgers, if the amount you receive exceeds £4,250 a year. Many social security benefits are also taxable. The tax year runs from 6 April to 5 April the following year, so the amount of tax you pay in any one year is calculated on the income you receive (or are deemed to have received) between these two dates.

At the time of writing, there are three different rates of income tax: the 10 per cent rate, which applies to the first £2,230 of your taxable income; the 22 per cent basic rate tax, which applies to the next slice of taxable income between £2,231 and £34,600; and the 40 per cent higher rate tax, which is levied on all taxable income over £34,600. All income tax payers will pay the 10 per cent rate on their first £2,230 of taxable income. Or put another way, for every £100 of your income that counts for income tax purposes up to £2,230, you have to pay £10 to the Exchequer – and are allowed to keep the remaining £90. If you are a basic-rate taxpayer, the amount you have to pay the Exchequer increases (after the first £2,230) to £22; and if you are a higher-rate taxpayer, it goes up to £40 for every £100 of your taxable income over £34,600.

The above figures applied to the 2007/08 tax year. Changes that came into effect from the start of the 2008/09 tax year include the basic rate of income tax being cut from 22 to 20 per cent. Also from 2008–09 there is a 10 per cent starting rate for savings income only, with a limit of £2,320. If your non-savings income is above this limit, then the 10 per cent starting rate for savings will not apply. There are no changes to the 10 per cent dividend ordinary rate or the 32.5 per cent dividend upper rate.

Another change that affects many earners' take-home pay is the increase in National Insurance contributions (NICs), which took effect in April 2008. Both the upper earnings limit for employees' Class 1 NIC and the Class 4 National Insurance upper profits limit, applicable to the self-employed, increased. In 2009 these limits will be aligned with the upper limit for basic rate income tax, making some people worse off.

Tax allowances

Personal allowance

You don't pay tax on every single penny of your money. You are allowed to retain a certain amount before income tax becomes applicable. This is known as your personal allowance. When calculating how much tax you will have to pay in any one year, first deduct from your total income the amount represented by your personal allowance. You should add any other tax allowance to which you may be entitled – see below. You will not have to pay any income tax if your income does not exceed your personal allowance (or total of your allowances).

Calculating your personal allowance used to be fairly complicated, as there were all sorts of variations. These depended on whether individuals were married or single, whether only one partner, or both husband and wife, worked. Since the introduction of independent taxation the system has become easier to understand. Today everyone receives the same basic personal allowance. This is regardless of whether they are male, female, married or single. It does not matter where the income comes from, whether they have earnings, an investment, their pension or other source.

■ The basic personal allowance (2008/09) is £6,035.

People aged 65 and over may be entitled to a higher personal allowance than the basic, by virtue of their age. Those aged 75 and above may receive even more generous treatment. The full allowance is only given to people whose income does not exceed £21,800. People with higher incomes may still receive some age-related allowance but this is gradually withdrawn by £1 for every £2 of income above the (£21,800) income limit. People with incomes above a certain level do not receive any age allowance. This ceiling is colloquially known as the upper limit. But however large your income, your personal allowance can never be reduced below the basic personal allowance.

For those aged 65 to 74:

▓ personal allowance is increased to £9,030;

▓ the upper limit is £28,990.

For those aged 75 and older:

▓ personal allowance is increased to £9,180;

▓ the upper limit is £29,290.

NB: Extra allowance linked to age is normally given automatically. If you are not receiving it but believe you should be doing so, contact your local tax office by phone, or speak to the HMRC general information line: Tel: 0845 9000 444; the HMRC website: www.hmrc.gov.uk, gives details. If you have been missing out, you may be able to claim back anything you have lost for up to six years and should receive a tax rebate. The amounts have been altered several times in recent years, so any rebate would only apply to allowances that would have been due to you at the time.

Married couple's allowance

Married couple's allowance was abolished, except for older couples, at the start of the April 2000/01 tax year. Those still entitled to receive the allowance are: 1) couples where at least one of the partners was born before 6 April 1935; and 2) older newly-weds, provided that one of the partners is aged 65 or more at the time of the marriage and that their date of birth was before 6 April 1935. In both cases, to be eligible, a couple must live together, as opposed to being separated.

Similar to the (age-related) personal allowance, couples whose income is below a set ceiling (the upper limit) are entitled to a higher allowance. This used to be known as age-related married couple's allowance because it always only applied to couples where either husband or wife was aged at least 65. This is still the case, except that for couples where neither partner has yet had a 75th birthday, income rather than age is now the only consideration. When either partner reaches 75, the allowance is increased, but, as before, only couples whose income is below the upper limit receive any extra.

A further point to note is that unlike the old basic married couple's allowance, which could be shared equally between the spouses or transferred in whole to the wife, the age/income-related addition always goes to the husband. If the husband has insufficient income against which to use all of the age/income addition, he should enquire at the tax office re the possibility of transferring the remainder to his wife. In the case of civil partners, the allowance is based on the income of the higher earner.

The current (2008/09) married couple's allowance, together with the income limits for the higher allowance, is as follows:

▪ The minimum married couple's allowance is £2,540.

▪ The higher income-related allowance for couples where both partners are under 75 is £6,535. The income limit to receive the full amount is £21,800. The upper limit is £28,990.

▪ When the husband or wife reaches 75, the allowance is increased to £6,625. The income limit stays at £21,800 and the upper limit is £29,290.

NB: Three important points you should know:

▪ Married couple's allowance is restricted to 10 per cent tax relief.

▪ The increases based on age/income are normally given automatically. If couples are not receiving any extra but believe they should be, the husband should contact their local tax office stating their ages. If there has been a mistake, he will be given a rebate.

▪ A widowed partner, where the couple at time of death were entitled to married couple's allowance, can claim any unused portion of the allowance in the year he or she became widowed.

Registered blind people can claim an allowance of £1,800 a year. If both husband and wife are registered as blind, they can each claim the allowance. It is called the Blind Person's Allowance. If you think you would be eligible, you should write to your local tax office with full relevant details of your situation. If you were entitled to receive the allowance earlier but for some reason missed out on doing so, you may be able to obtain a tax rebate.

Useful reading

For more detailed information about tax allowances, see the following HMRC leaflets obtainable free from any tax office; their general advice helpline is: Tel: 0845 9000 444, or check the HMRC website: www.hmrc.gov.uk.

IR 121 *Income Tax and Pensioners*.

Rates and Allowances 2008/09.

Tax relief

Separate from any personal allowances, you can obtain tax relief on the following:

▨ a covenant for the benefit of a charity, or a donation under the Gift Aid Scheme;

▨ contributions to occupational pensions, self-employed pension plans and other personal pensions;

▨ some maintenance payments, if you are divorced or separated and were aged 65 or older on 5 April 2000.

Mortgage interest relief. As most home owners will know, mortgage interest relief was abolished on 6 April 2000. The only purpose for which relief is still available is in respect of loans secured on an older person's home to purchase a life annuity. However, to qualify the loan must have been taken out (or at least processed and confirmed in writing) by 9 March 1999. Borrowers in this situation can continue to benefit from the relief for the duration of their loan. As before, the relief remains at 10 per cent on the first £30,000 of the loan.

Maintenance payments. Tax relief for maintenance payments was also withdrawn on 6 April 2000. Individuals in receipt of maintenance payments are not affected and will continue to receive their money free of income tax. Those who had to pay tax under the pre-March 1988 rules now also receive their payments free of tax. Most individuals paying maintenance, however, face higher tax bills. This applies especially to those who set up arrangements before the March 1988 budget. Whereas previously they got tax relief at their highest rate, since 6 April 2000 when maintenance relief was withdrawn, they no longer get any relief at all. An exception has been made in cases where one, or both, of the divorced/separated spouses was aged 65 or over on 5 April 2000. Those paying maintenance are still able to claim tax relief – but only at the 1999/2000 standard rate of 10 per cent.

Pension contributions. HMRC sets limits on the contributions that individuals can invest in their pension plan and on the pension benefits they can receive. Individuals can invest up to 100 per cent of annual earnings into their plan (or plans) with the benefit of tax relief up to a maximum figure

– known as the annual allowance – of £225,000. Higher contributions are allowed but without any tax relief on the excess. If you have a stakeholder or personal pension, you can make contributions of up to £3,600 a year irrespective of your earnings (or even if you earn nothing at all). You pay the contributions net of basic rate tax and your pension provider will then reclaim the tax from HMRC.

The annual allowance is not the only capped amount. There is also a lifetime limit of £1.6 million for total pension funds, including any fund growth. Funds in excess of the lifetime limit are subject to a 25 per cent recovery charge (ie tax) if taken as income, or 55 per cent if taken as a lump sum. Both the annual allowance and the lifetime limit will be increased in stages, rising respectively to £255,000 and £1.8 million by 2010/11.

Fund protection. Individuals whose pension fund was already over the lifetime limit before 6 April 2006 – or anticipated to become so before they draw their pension – can protect their fund from the recovery charge, provided the fund is formally registered with HMRC within three years of 6 April 2006 (A-day).

There are two types of protection: standard (or primary) protection and enhanced protection. If your fund was already over the £1.5 million limit by A-day, you may do better to register for standard protection, as the amount you register will be expressed as a percentage of the lifetime limit (eg, if you had £3 million at A-day, it will be valued at 200 per cent of the annual limit, whatever that might be when you draw your pension benefits). Alternatively, if your fund was below the limit, enhanced protection has the advantage of protecting any further growth in the fund, but neither you nor an employer would have been able to make any further contributions into the scheme since 6 April 2006.

Tax-free lump sum. A further major change concerns the tax-free lump sum. As opposed to a maximum of one-and-a-half times final salary, which used to be the rule for members of company schemes, everyone (provided the scheme rules permit) is entitled to take up to 25 per cent of the value of their fund or 25 per cent of their lifetime limit, whichever is lower. Additional voluntary contributions (AVCs) and the opted-out benefits from the State Second Pension can count towards the lump sum instead of, as before, having to remain in the fund to provide pension income.

There is no longer any requirement for members of company schemes to wait until they retire before accessing their lump sum. Should they wish to do so, they can now take the money at any time from the age of 50. Members of final salary schemes cannot take their lump sum in isolation. A further point is that the minimum age for drawing the tax-free lump sum will rise from 50 to 55 in 2010. There is now also greater flexibility for employees nearing retirement who, as well as taking their tax-free lump sum, can also (provided their scheme rules allow) start drawing some pension income while still remaining at work part-time.

Scheme rules. The fact that HMRC has changed the rules is unfortunately no guarantee that individuals will be able to take full advantage of all the new options that have become available. Their employer's pension scheme rules will also need to have been altered accordingly, which may not always be the case. Before making any definite plans, it would first be advisable to check with whoever is responsible for the company pension scheme.

Pension Credit

Pension Credit is a means-tested state benefit for those over 60, giving certain pensioners extra money each week. It's made up of two elements – the 'Guarantee Credit' element and the 'Savings Credit' element. The Guarantee Credit is of benefit to single people with incomes of below £124.05 a week and to couples with incomes of below £189.35. The Savings Credit element applies to you if you're single and your total weekly income from money from savings, earnings and investments is between £91.20 and £174.00 per week, or if you have a partner, your joint weekly income from similar sources is between £145.80 and £255.00 per week. You may get more Pension Credit if you have caring responsibilities, are severely disabled or have certain housing costs.

From 6 October 2008 some important changes have taken place to Pension Credit. From that date, when someone applies over the phone for Pension Credit and, at the same time, for housing and council tax benefits, the Pension Service will automatically send their claim information to the appropriate local authority. This does away with the need for another claim form to be completed and signed. Also, claimants are now able to spend up to 13 weeks abroad (increased from four weeks) and still retain entitlement to Pension Credit. This brings the benefit into line with housing and council tax benefits. Probably the most important change is that the backdating of Pension Credit claims is limited to three months, again bringing it into line with other benefits. Previously arrears were backdated for up to 12 months.

If you require further information, you can call the Pension Credit helpline on 0800 99 1234 who will give you advice on whether your income and/or capital meet the necessary conditions for a successful claim. You can also look at the website: www.direct.gov.uk.

Tax-free income

Some income you may receive is entirely free of tax – it is not taxed at source and you do not have to deduct it from your income, as in the case of personal allowances. Nor do you have to go through the formality of claiming relief on it. If you receive any of the following, you can forget about the tax aspect altogether – at least as regards these particular items:

▦ disability living allowance;

▦ industrial injuries disablement pension;

▦ income support (in some circumstances, such as when the recipient is also getting jobseeker's allowance, income support benefit would be taxable);

▦ housing benefit;

■ council tax benefit;

■ all pensions paid to war widows (plus any additions for children);

■ pensions paid to victims of Nazism;

■ certain disablement pensions from the armed forces, police, fire brigade and merchant navy;

■ annuities paid to the holders of certain gallantry awards;

■ £10 Christmas bonus (paid to pensioners);

■ National Savings Premium Bond prizes;

■ SAYE bonuses;

■ winnings on the football pools and on other forms of betting;

■ rental income of up to £4,250 a year from letting out rooms in your home;

■ winter fuel payment (paid to pensioners);

■ the extra £400 winter fuel payment paid to households with a resident aged 80 and over;

■ income received from certain insurance policies (mort-gage payment protection, permanent health insurance, creditor insurance for loans and utility bills, various approved long-term care policies) if the recipient is sick, disabled or unemployed at the time the benefits become payable;

- all income received from savings in an ISA (Individual Savings Account);

- all dividend income from investments in VCTs (Venture Capital Trusts).

Other tax-free money

The following are not income, in the sense that they are more likely to be 'one off' rather than regular payments. However, as with the above list they are tax-free:

- Virtually all gifts (in certain circumstances you could have to pay tax if the gift is above £3,000 or if, as may occasionally be the case, the money from the donor has not been previously taxed).

- Redundancy payment, or a golden handshake in lieu of notice, up to the value of £30,000;

- Lump sum commuted from a pension.

- A matured endowment policy.

- Accumulated interest from a Tax Exempt Special Savings Account (TESSA) held for five years.

▓ Dividends on investments held in a Personal Equity Plan (PEP).

▓ Compensation money paid to people who were mis-sold personal pensions.

▓ Compensation paid to those who were mis-sold free-standing AVCs (FSAVCs). To qualify for exemption from tax, the money must be paid as a lump sum as opposed to in annual payments.

Income tax on savings

In 2008/09 the 10 per cent starting rate on income tax was abolished for earned and pensions income, though does remain for savings income and capital gains. If you largely rely on your savings income and so believe you are among those who are or have been paying excess tax, you can reclaim this from HM Revenue & Customs. For advice on what to do, call the **Taxback helpline** on: Tel: 0845 077 6543 (calls charged at local rates) or see the HMRC website: www.hmrc.gov.uk. You might also find it useful to see 'Reclaiming tax overpaid', page 20.

Income tax on other investments

For most investments on which you are likely to receive dividends, basic-rate tax will already have been deducted before the money is paid to you. If you are a basic-rate taxpayer, the money you receive will be yours in its entirety and you will not have to make deductions for tax. If you pay tax at the higher rate, you will have to pay some additional tax and should allow for this in your budgeting.

Exceptionally, there are a few types of investment where the money is paid to you gross – without the basic-rate tax deducted. These include NS&I income bonds, capital bonds, the NS&I Investment Account – and all gilt interest. (People who prefer to receive gilt interest net can opt to do so.) As with higher-rate taxpayers, you will need to save sufficient money to pay the tax on the due date.

Avoiding paying excess tax on savings income

Banks and building societies automatically deduct the normal 20 per cent rate of tax from interest before it is paid to savers. As a result most working people, except higher-rate taxpayers, can keep all their savings without having to worry about paying additional tax. Although convenient for the majority, a problem is that some four million people on low incomes – including in particular many women and pensioners – are unwittingly paying more tax than they need. Those most affected are non-taxpayers (anyone whose taxable income is less than their allowances) who, although not liable for tax, are having it taken from their income before they receive the money.

Non-taxpayers can stop this happening quite simply by requesting their bank and/or building society to pay any interest owing to them gross, without deduction of tax at source. If applicable, all you need do is to request form R85 from the institution in question or HMRC Enquiry Centre, which you will then need to complete. If you have more than one bank or building society account, you will need a separate form for each account. People who have filled in an R85 should automatically receive their interest gross. If your form was not completed in time for this to happen, you can reclaim the tax from your tax office after the end of the tax year in April.

Reclaiming tax overpaid

If you are a non-taxpayer and have not yet completed an R85 form (or forms), you are very likely to be eligible to claim a tax rebate. However, as stated earlier, this may also apply if you only pay tax at the 10 per cent starting rate; or if, since becoming retired, most of your income now comes from either taxed investments or bank/building society interest. If any of these circumstances apply and you believe that the probability is that you could be due a refund, best advice is to ring the special **Taxback Helpline** on Tel: 0845 077 6543; they will send you a claim form and, if relevant, copies of form R85 for you to complete and give to your bank/building society.

If you had not realised that the tax could be deducted and so had not requested an R85 form, or if despite having given your bank/building society a completed form, they had forgotten to deduct the tax, you can ask the Taxback Helpline to send you form R40M, which once completed will enable your bank/building society to refund you any overpaid tax for up to six years.

Mistakes by HM Revenue & Customs (HMRC)

HM Revenue & Customs do sometimes make mistakes. Normally, if they have charged you insufficient tax and later discover the error, they will send you a supplementary demand requesting the balance owing. However, under a provision known as the 'Official Error Concession', if the mistake was due to HMRC's failure 'to make proper and timely use' of information it received, it is possible that you may be excused the arrears. For this to be likely, you would need to convince HMRC that you could reasonably have believed that your tax affairs were in order. Additionally, HMRC itself would need to have been tardy in notifying you of the arrears: this would normally mean more than 12 months after the end of the tax year in which HMRC received the information indicating that more tax was due.

Undercharging is not the only type of error. It is equally possible that you may have been overcharged and either do not owe as much as has been stated or, not having spotted the mistake, paid more than you needed to. As part of the Citizen's Charter, HMRC has appointed an independent Adjudicator to examine taxpayers' complaints about their dealings with HMRC and, if considered valid, to determine what action would be fair. Complaints appropriate to the Adjudicator are mainly limited to the way HMRC has handled someone's tax affairs. Before approaching the Adjudicator, taxpayers are expected to have tried to resolve the matter, either with their local tax office or, should that fail, with the regional office.

HMRC is, however, getting tougher about mistakes where, for whatever reason, there is an understatement of the amount of tax due. Genuine mistakes will still be excused but individuals may need to convince officials that they had not been careless in completing their return. Otherwise they could be at risk of incurring a penalty. More immediately, the deadline for filing paper self-assessment forms for the 2008/09 tax year is 31 October 2009. Those filing online will have until 31 January 2010.

For further information, see HMRC booklet, Code of Practice 1, *Putting Things Right. How to Complain*, available from tax offices. Contact the Adjudicator's Office for information about referring a complaint. The Adjudicator acts as a fair and unbiased referee looking into complaints about HMRC, including the Tax Credit Office, the Valuation Office and the Office of the Public Guardian and The Insolvency Service. **The Adjudicator's Office**: Tel: 0300 057 1111; website: www.adjudicatorsoffice.gov.uk.

Other useful organisations

Taxpayers' Alliance has a campaign team of energetic volunteers committed to achieving a low-tax society. It has over 18,000 supporters and is regularly mentioned in the media. For further information, contact: Tel: 0845 330 9554; email: info@taxpayersalliance.com; website: www.tpa.type pad.com.

Tax Help for Older People is an independent free tax-advice service for older people on low incomes who cannot afford to pay for professional advice. If your household income is less than £15,000 a year and you are a pensioner you will qualify for free tax advice from TOP. This organisation offers the service originally provided through the Low Incomes Tax Reform Group. For further information, contact: Tel: 0845 601 3321; email: taxvol@taxvol.org.uk; website: www.taxvol.org.uk.

Tax rebates

When you retire, you may be due for a tax rebate. If you are, this would normally be paid automatically, especially if you are getting a pension from your last employer. The matter could conceivably be overlooked, either if you are due to get a pension from an earlier employer (instead of from your last employer), or if you will only be receiving a State pension – and not a company pension in addition.

In either case, you should ask your employer for a P45 form. Then, either send it – care of your earlier employer – to the pension fund trustees or, in the event of your only receiving a State pension, send it to the tax office together with details of your age and the date you retired. Ask your employer for the address of the tax office to which you should write. If the repayment is made to you more than a year after the end of the year for which the repayment is due – and is more than £25 – HMRC will automatically pay you (tax-free) interest. HMRC calls this 'Repayment Supplement'.

Post-war credits

Post-war credits are extra tax that people had to pay in addition to their income tax between April 1941 and April 1946. The extra tax was treated as a credit to be repaid after the war. People who paid credits were given certificates showing the amount actually paid. Repayment started in 1946, initially only to men aged 65 or over and to women aged 60 or over, but the conditions for claiming varied over the years until 1972, when it was announced that there would be a 'general release' and that all credits were to be repaid without any further restrictions. In 1972 people who could produce at least one of their post-war credit certificates were invited to claim. In cases where the original credit holder has died without claiming repayment and the post-war credit certificate is still available, repayment can be made to the next of kin or personal representative of the estate. Interest is payable on all claims at a composite rate of 38 per cent. The interest is exempt from income tax. All claims should be sent to the **Special Post-War Credit Claim Centre** at: HM Revenue & Customs, HM Inspector of Taxes – PWC Centre V, Ty Glas, Llanishen, Cardiff CF4 5TX; Tel: 0845 300 3949.

Capital gains tax (CGT)

You may have to pay capital gains tax if you make a profit (or to use the proper term, gain) on the sale of a capital asset; for example, stocks and shares, jewellery, any property that is not your main home and other items of value. CGT only applies to the actual gain you make, so if you buy shares to the value of £100,000 and sell them later for £125,000 the tax officer will only be interested in the £25,000 profit you have made.

Not all your gains are taxable. There is an **exemption limit of £9,600** (2008/09) a year: so if during the year your total gains amount to £14,500, tax would only be levied on £4,900.

A very important point for married couples to know is that as a result of independent taxation each partner now enjoys his/her own annual exemption of £9,600 instead of, as before, their gains being aggregated (ie added together) for tax purposes. This means in effect that, provided both partners are taking advantage of their full exemption limit, a couple can make gains of £19,200 a year free of CGT. However, it is not possible to use the losses of one spouse to cover the gains of the other. Transfers between husband and wife remain tax-free, although any income arising from such a gift will of course be taxed. Income would normally be treated as the recipient's for tax purposes.

Gains made before April 2008 are taxed at the same rate as your income: 10 per cent where the gains fall below the starting rate limit for income tax of £2,230; 20 per cent where they fall between the starting rate and basic rate limits for income tax, ie, between £2,331 and £34,600; or at 40 per cent where they fall above the basic rate limit for income tax, ie, £34,601 and above. However, for gains made since April 2008, you are charged at a flat 18 per cent.

Taper relief was abolished in April 2008 when the Capital Gains Tax system was reformed. It was overhauled so that private equity firms would pay a fairer share of tax. The new single rate of 18 per cent tax rate applies across the board. But a new entrepreneurs' relief will reduce the effective tax rate on some gains to 10 per cent.

Free of capital gains tax

The following assets are not subject to CGT and do not count towards the £9,600 gains you are allowed to make:

■ your main home (but, see 'Your home' below);

■ your car;

■ personal belongings up to the value of £6,000 each;

■ proceeds of a life assurance policy (in most circumstances);

■ profits on UK Government stocks;

■ National Savings Certificates;

■ SAYE contracts;

■ building society mortgage cash backs;

■ futures and options in gilts and qualifying corporate bonds;

■ Personal Equity Plan (PEP) schemes;

- gains from assets held in an Individual Savings Account (ISA);

- Premium Bond winnings;

- football pool and other bettings winnings;

- gifts to registered charities;

- small part disposals of land (limited to 5 per cent of the total holding, with a maximum value of £20,000);

- gains on the disposal of qualifying shares in a Venture Capital Trust (VCT) or within the Enterprise Investment Scheme (EIS), provided these have been held for the necessary holding period (see below).

The **Enterprise Investment Scheme (EIS)** allows individuals investing in qualifying unquoted companies 20 per cent income tax relief on investments up to £400,000 and exemption from capital gains tax on disposal of the shares, provided these have been held for at least three years. Losses qualify for income tax or CGT relief. A further advantage is that whereas deferral relief has been withdrawn in respect of VCTs since 6 April 2004, those investing in an EIS can still defer any CGT liability, provided gains are invested in qualifying unquoted companies within three years. Also, an investor can become a paid director, provided he/she was not connected with the company at time of the first investment. For further information, visit the HMRC website: www.hmrc.gov.uk.

Your home. Your main home is usually exempt from CGT. However, there are certain 'ifs and buts' that could be important. If you convert part of your home into an office or into self-contained accommodation on which you charge rent, the part of your home that is deemed to be a 'business' may be separately assessed – and CGT may be payable when you come to sell it. (CGT would not apply if you simply take in a lodger who is treated as family, in the sense of sharing your kitchen or bathroom.)

If you leave your home to someone else who later decides to sell it, then he/she may be liable for CGT when the property is sold (although only on the gain since the date of death). There may also be inheritance tax implications, so if you are thinking of leaving or giving your home to someone, you are strongly advised to consult a solicitor or accountant. If you own two homes, only one of them is exempt from CGT, namely the one you designate as your 'main residence'.

Selling a family business. Taper relief (as previously stated) was abolished in April 2008; the CGT now payable if you are selling a family business is 18 per cent. One possible option is the CGT deferral relief allowable to investors in an EIS. Investors – including entrepreneur owner/directors with gains arising from the sale of shares in their own companies – can defer paying CGT and in many cases can also obtain income tax relief at 20 per cent on investments of up to £400,000 a year, provided gains are reinvested in qualifying unquoted companies (including AIM and Ofex companies) within three years.

In recent years, some of the rules have been altered to create a more unified system of venture capital reliefs. This is a very complex field, so before either retiring or selling shares, you are strongly recommended to seek professional advice.

Useful reading

For further information about capital gains tax, see booklet CGT 1, *Capital Gains Tax: An introduction*, available from any tax office. Consult the HMRC website: www.hmrc. gov.uk.

Inheritance tax

Inheritance tax (IHT) applies to money and/or gifts with a capital value passed on at time of death (or sometimes before). New IHT rules came into effect as from 9 October 2007.

For the tax year 2008–09, the first £312,000 of an individual's estate is tax-free. For married couples and civil partners it is £624,000. For 2009–10 it will be £325,000 for individuals or £650,000 for married couples and civil partners. For 2010–11 it will be £350,000 for individuals or £700,000 for married couples and civil partners. The value of estates over and above the allowance is taxed at 40 per cent. The proportion of estates forecast to pay inheritance tax in 2008–09 is 5 per cent.

Before any tax is calculated, there are a number of exemptions and other concessions that may be relevant. There is no immediate tax on lifetime gifts between individuals. The gifts become wholly exempt if the donor survives for seven years. When the donor dies, any gifts made within the previous seven years become chargeable and their value is added to that of the estate. The total is then taxed on the excess over £312,000. Chargeable gifts benefit first towards the £312,000 exemption, starting with the earliest gifts and continuing in the order in which they were given. Any unused balance of the £312,000 threshold goes towards the remaining estate.

Under the new rules the £312,000 threshold has not increased but married couples are now able to transfer the unused element of their IHT-free allowance to their spouse when they die. For many couples this effectively doubles the tax-free amount they can bequeath to their children. In practice it will work along the following lines: if a husband dies and leaves all his assets to his wife, she will be able to bequeath up to £624,000 tax-free to her children. The £624,000 is made up of her and her late husband's joint IHT-free £312,000 allowances. Widows and widowers will be able to benefit because the rules will be back-dated indefinitely, so any widows or widowers will be able to use their late partner's IHT-free allowance as well as their own when they die. IHT will, however, still be levied at 40 per cent above £312,000 on the estate of anyone who is single or divorced when they die.

Gifts or money up to the value of £3,000 can also be given annually free of tax, regardless of the particular date they were given. Additionally, it is possible to make small gifts to any number of individuals free of tax, provided the amount to each does not exceed £250.

Although most ex-owners or their heirs will end up paying one way or another, the Chancellor has built in certain exclusions and exemptions, including preserving the important principle that transfers of property between spouses remain exempt from any tax. Tax will equally not be charged if the asset is sold for full market value or if, due to a change in circumstances, an owner who had previously given away a property needs to reoccupy his or her former home.

Quite apart from IHT, capital gains tax may have to be paid on any asset you left to a beneficiary, or as part of your estate, which is subsequently sold. HM Revenue & Customs treats such assets as having been acquired at the date of death and at their prevailing market value at the time. By the same token, CGT will have to be paid on any gain that has built up on an asset you gave away during your lifetime and that is subsequently sold.

Another important consideration that should not be overlooked is the need to make a will. The rules of intestacy are very rigid and neglecting to make a proper will can have serious consequences for those whom you might wish to benefit. For further information, see Chapter 4 (Wills, page 101).

Tax treatment of trusts. Under the new rules for aligning the inheritance tax treatment for trusts, those who have set up or have an interest in "accumulation & maintenance" trusts (A&Ms) and/or "interest in possession" trusts (IIPs) that do not meet new inheritance tax (IHT) rules about their terms and the circumstances in which they are created are most affected. The new rules came into effect on 22 March 2006 for new trusts, additions of new assets to existing trusts and for other IHT relevant events in relation to existing trusts. Transitional rules provided for a period of adjustment for certain existing trusts to 6 April 2008.

Discretionary trusts are assessed for IHT on their tenth anniversary and every 10 years thereafter. Distributions from the trust may also trigger an IHT charge. These rules apply to trusts created during the settlor's lifetime and those created within the settlor's will. Following proposals announced in the March 2006 Budget Statement, the same treatment will apply to funds gifted on or after 22 March 2006 into most interest in possession (IIP) and accumulation and maintenance (A&M) trusts.

This is a particularly complex area and professional advice is recommended. Further information is available from the Probate/IHT Helpline on: Tel: 0845 30 20 900; website: www.hmcourts-service.gov.uk.

Independent taxation

The introduction of independent taxation in April 1990 affected nearly all married couples. As well as allowing married women privacy in their own financial affairs, another major gain was that many couples – especially retired people – became better off financially. In contrast to the old system, whereby a married woman's income was treated as belonging to her husband for taxation purposes, both husband and wife are now taxed independently on their own income. Each has his/her own personal allowance and rate band; and both independently pay their own tax and receive their own tax rebates. Moreover, independent taxation applies equally to the age-related additions and both husband and wife are now eligible for their own higher tax allowance from the age of 65 (and a more generous allowance still after age 75).

A further important point for many couples is that independent taxation does not simply apply to income tax but applies equally to both capital gains tax and inheritance tax. As a result, both husband and wife enjoy their own capital gains tax exemption (£9,600 in the 2008/09 tax year) and their own exemption from inheritance tax (£312,000 in the 2008/09 tax year). Property left to a surviving spouse remains, as before, free of inheritance tax.

Useful reading

Zurich Tax Handbook 2008–2009 – ISBN 9780 2737 2143 7. Available from Pearson: website: www.pearsoned.co.uk; Tel: 01279 623928. Price £34.99 plus p&p.

HMRC leaflets that could be helpful, especially if you are interested in the possibility of becoming self-employed or starting your own business, include: SE1 *Thinking of Working for Yourself?* and IR56 *Employed or Self-Employed? A Guide to Employment Status for Tax and National Insurance.*

Self-assessment

If you are one of the nine million people who need to complete a tax return, you will probably be all too familiar with self-assessment. The tax return forms are sent out in April. If you have not already done so, the details you need to enter on the form you received in April 2008 are those relating to the 2007/08 tax year. The details you need to enter on the form you receive in April 2009 are those relating to the 2008/09 tax year.

Even if you have never had a tax return, so are unlikely to be directly affected by self-assessment unless your circumstances change, all taxpayers now have a legal obligation to keep records of all their different sources of income and capital gains. These include:

▓ details of your earnings plus any bonus, expenses and benefits in kind you received;

▓ bank and building society interest;

▓ dividend vouchers and/or other documentation showing gains from investments;

▓ pension payments, ie both State and occupational/ private pension;

▓ miscellaneous income, such as freelance earnings, maintenance payments, taxable social security benefits;

▓ payments against which you claim tax relief (eg charitable donations, contributions to a personal pension).

HMRC advises that you are obliged to keep these records for 22 months after the end of the tax year to which they relate.

If you are self-employed or a partner in a business, as well as the above list you also need to keep records of all your business earnings and expenses, together with sales invoices and receipts. All records (both personal and business) need to be kept for five years after the fixed filing date. Those most likely to be affected by the self-assessment system include anyone who normally receives a tax return, higher-rate taxpayers, company directors, the self-employed and partners in a business.

If your only income is from your salary from which tax is deducted at source, you will not have to worry about self-assessment. If, however, you have other income that is not fully taxed under PAYE (eg benefits in kind or expenses payments) or that is not fully taxed at source, you need to notify HM Revenue & Customs within six months of the end of the tax year and you may need to fill in a tax return.

A very important point to know for anyone who might be feeling worried is that self-calculation is optional. If you think the calculations are too complicated or that you might be at risk of making a mistake, HMRC will continue as before to do the sums for you. Until recently, tax payers who wanted HMRC to calculate their tax liability for them had to file their return by an earlier date. Today, this is no longer an issue. Instead, what matters is whether you file online or submit a paper return. Paper returns must be filed by 31 October each year; the deadline for online filing is 31 January the following year.

For further information, see booklets SA/BK4 *Self-assessment – A general guide to keeping records*; SA/BK6 *Self-assessment – Penalties for late tax returns*; SA/BK7 *Self-assessment – Surcharges for late payment of tax* and SA/BK8 *Self- assessment – Your guide*, all obtainable free from any tax office. You can also call the **Self-assessment**

Helpline on: Tel: 0845 900 0444; website: www.direct.gov. uk. HMRC website: www.hmrc.gov.uk.

Retiring abroad

There are many examples of people who retired abroad in the expectation of being able to afford a higher standard of living and who returned home a few years later, thoroughly disillusioned. As with other important decisions, this is where it is essential to thoroughly research your options. It is crucial to investigate property prices as well as, of course, the cost of health care. As anyone who has ever needed a doctor or dentist abroad knows, the term 'free health service' does not always mean what it says. Although these and similar points are perhaps obvious, a vital question that is often overlooked is the taxation effects of living overseas. If you are thinking of retiring abroad, do look into this before you go.

Taxation abroad

Tax rates vary from one country to another: a prime example is VAT, which varies considerably in Europe. Additionally, many countries levy taxes that don't apply to Britain. Wealth tax exists in quite a few parts of the world. Estate duty on property left by one spouse to another is also fairly widespread. If you are thinking of retiring abroad the golden rule must be to investigate the situation thoroughly before you take an irrevocable step, such as selling your home. However, an even more common mistake is to misunderstand your UK tax liabilities after your departure.

Your UK tax position if you retire overseas

Many intending emigrants cheerfully imagine that once they have settled themselves in a dream villa overseas, they are safely out of the clutches of the UK tax office. This is not so. You first have to acquire non-resident status. If you have severed all your ties, including selling your home, to take up a permanent job overseas, this is normally granted fairly quickly. But for most retirees, acquiring unconditional non-resident status can take up to three years. The purpose is to check that you are not just having a prolonged holiday but are actually living as a resident abroad. During the check period, HM Revenue & Customs may allow you conditional non-resident status; and if they are satisfied, full status will be granted retrospectively.

Rules. The rules for non-residency are pretty stringent. You are not allowed:

▪ to spend more than 182 days in the United Kingdom in any one tax year; or

▪ to spend more than an average of 90 days per year in the United Kingdom over a maximum of four tax years.

Even if you are not resident in the United Kingdom, some of your income may still be liable for UK taxation.

Income tax

▪ All overseas income (provided it is not remitted to the United Kingdom) is exempt from UK tax liability.

▦ Income deriving from a UK source is, however, normally liable for UK tax. This includes any director's or consultant's fees you may still be receiving, as well as more obvious income such as rent from a property you still own.

▦ An exception may be made if the country in which you have taken up residency has a double tax agreement with the United Kingdom (see below). If this is the case, you may be taxed on the income in your new residence – and not in the United Kingdom.

▦ Additionally, interest paid on certain British Government securities is not subject to tax.

▦ Non-residents may be able to arrange for their interest on a British bank deposit or building society account to be paid gross.

▦ Some former colonial pensions are also exempted.

Double tax agreement. A person who is a resident of a country with which the United Kingdom has a double taxation agreement may be entitled to exemption or partial relief from UK income tax on certain kinds of income from UK sources and may also be exempt from UK tax on the disposal of assets. The conditions of exemption or relief vary from agreement to agreement. It may be a condition of the relief that the income is subject to tax in the other country. **NB:** If, as sometimes happens, the foreign tax authority later makes an adjustment and the income ceases to be taxed in that country, you have an obligation under the self-assessment rules to notify HM Revenue & Customs.

Capital gains tax (CGT)

This is only charged if you are resident or ordinarily resident in the United Kingdom; so if you are in the position of being able to realise a gain, it is advisable to wait until you acquire non-resident status. However, to escape CGT, you must wait to dispose of any assets until after the tax year of your departure and must remain non-resident (and not ordinarily resident) in the United Kingdom for five full tax years after your departure. Different rules apply to gains made from the disposal of assets in a UK company. These are subject to normal CGT.

Inheritance tax (IHT)

You only escape tax if: 1) you were domiciled overseas for all of the immediate three years prior to death; 2) you were resident overseas for more than three tax years in your final 20 years of life; and 3) all your assets were overseas. Even if you have been resident overseas for many years, if you do not have an overseas domicile, you will have to pay IHT at the same rates as if you lived in the United Kingdom.

Domicile. Broadly speaking, you are domiciled in the country in which you have your permanent home. Domicile is distinct from nationality or residence. A person may be resident in more than one country but at any given time he/she can only be domiciled in one. If you are resident in a country and intend to spend the rest of your days there, it could be sensible to decide to change your domicile. If, however, you are resident but there is a chance that you might move, the country where you are living would not qualify as your domicile. This is a complicated area, where professional advice is recommended if you are contemplating a change.

UK pensions paid abroad

▨ Any queries about your pension should be addressed to the International Payments Office, **International Pensions Centre:** Tel: 0191 218 7777; website: www.the pensionservice.gov.uk.

▨ Technically your State pension could be subject to income tax, as it derives from the United Kingdom. In practice, if this is your only source of UK income, tax would be unlikely to be charged.

▨ If you have an occupational pension, UK tax will normally be charged on the total of the two amounts.

▨ Both State and occupational pensions may be paid to you in any country. If you are planning to retire to Australia, Canada, New Zealand or South Africa, you would be advised to check on the up-to-date position regarding any annual increases you would expect to receive to your pension. Some people have found the level of their pension 'frozen' at the date they left Britain, whereas others have been liable for unexpected tax overseas.

▨ If the country where you are living has a double tax agreement with the United Kingdom, as previously explained, your income may be taxed there – and not in Great Britain. Britain now has a double tax agreement with most countries. For further information, check the position with your local tax office.

▓ If your pension is taxed in the United Kingdom, you will be able to claim your personal allowance as an offset. A married man living with his wife may also be able to claim the married couple's allowance, if by virtue of their age they would still be eligible to receive it (see 'Married couple's allowance', page 8).

Health care overseas

People retiring to another EU country before State retirement age can apply to DWP Overseas Contributions for a form E106, which will entitle them to State health care in that country on the same basis as local people. An E106 is only valid for a maximum of two-and-a-half years, after which it is usually necessary to take out private insurance cover until State retirement age is reached. Thereafter, UK pensioners can request the International Pensions Centre (see above) for a form E121, entitling them and their dependants to State health care as provided by the country in which they are living.

Useful reading

Residents and Non Residents – Liability to tax in the UK (IR 20), available from any tax office.

Leaflet SA29, *Your Social Security Insurance, Benefits and Health Care Rights in the European Community*, contains essential information about what to do if you retire to another EU country. Available from any social security or Jobcentre Plus office: website: www.jobcentreplus. gov.uk.

2

Investments

Investment is a subject for everyone. One of your single most important aims must be to make your existing money work for you so you will be more comfortable in the years ahead. The younger you start planning the better. If you are already 65 or over, there is still plenty you can do.

Your investment strategy must be aimed not just for your 60s and 70s but also for your 80s, or even your 90s.

Inflation is another essential factor that must be taken into account. People on fixed incomes are the hardest hit when inflation rises. Even when inflation rates are low it takes its toll to an alarming extent. The current economic climate is affecting many people adversely, not least savers.

Sources of investable funds

You may have some money for investment. Possible sources of quite significant capital include:

▨ Commuted lump sum from your pension. There is now one set of rules for all types of pension scheme, with members allowed a maximum of 25 per cent of their pension fund or 25 per cent of their lifetime limit, whichever is lower. There is no tax to pay when you receive the money.

▨ Insurance policies designed to mature around your retirement. These are normally tax free.

▨ Profits on your home, if you sell it and move to smaller, less-expensive accommodation. Provided this is your main home, there is no capital gains tax to pay.

▨ Redundancy money, golden handshake or other farewell gift from your employer. You are allowed £30,000 redundancy money free of tax. The same is usually true of other severance pay up to £30,000, but there can be tax if, however worded, your employment contract indicates that these are deferred earnings.

▨ Sale of SAYE and other share option schemes. The tax rules vary according to the type of scheme, the date the options were acquired and how long the shares have been held before disposal. Since the rules are liable to change with each Budget statement, for further information, contact: HMRC at www.hmrc.gov.uk.

General investment strategy

Investments differ in their aims, tax treatment and the amount of risk involved. One or two categories are only suitable for the very rich, who can afford to take more significant risks. Others, such as certain types of National Savings, are only really suitable for those on a very low income.

These two groups apart, the aim for most people should be to acquire a balanced portfolio: in other words, a mix of investments variously designed to provide some income to supplement your pension and also some capital appreciation to maintain your standard of living in the long term.

Except for annuities, National Savings and Investments and property, which have sections to themselves, the different types of investment are listed by groups, as follows:

- variable-interest accounts;

- fixed-interest securities;

- equities;

- long-term lock-ups.

As a general strategy, it is a good idea to aim to choose at least one type of investment from each group.

Annuities

Definition. A normal life annuity is a very simple investment to understand. You pay a capital sum to an insurance company and in return are guaranteed a fixed income for life. The money is paid to you at fixed intervals and will remain exactly the same year in, year out. Payments are calculated according to life expectancy tables, and for this reason an annuity may not really be a suitable investment for anyone under 70. Other than your age, the key factor affecting the amount you will receive in payments is the level of interest rates at the time you buy: the higher these are, the more you will receive.

An annuity would probably give you more immediate income than any other form of investment. But whether you actually get good value depends on how long you live. When you die, your capital will be gone and there will be no more payments. So if you die a short while after signing the contract, it will represent very bad value indeed. On the other hand, if you live a very long time, you may more than recoup your original capital. As a precaution against early death, it is possible to take out one of three types of annuity.

The difference between the three choices is briefly as follows. **Capital protected annuities** pay out any balance left from your original investment after deduction of the gross annuity payments paid to date. **Annuities with a guarantee period** are normal life annuities with the important difference that if you die before the end of the guaranteed period, the payments for the remaining years (of the guaranteed period) will go to your partner or other beneficiary. **Annuities incorporating a spouse's benefit** pay out the annuity income to you during your lifetime and will then pass to your partner for the remainder of his/her life.

Tax. Income tax on optional annuities is relatively low, as part of the income is allowed as a return on capital that is not taxable. Pension-linked annuities are fully taxable.

How to obtain. You can buy an annuity either direct from an insurance company or via an intermediary, such as an independent financial adviser (IFA). But shop around, since, as mentioned above, the payments vary considerably. To find an IFA, contact: **IFA Promotion Ltd:** Tel: 0800 085 3250; email: contact@ifap.org.uk; or consult their website: www.unbiased.co.uk.

Assessment. Safe; attractive if you live to a ripe old age; but highly vulnerable to inflation. Sacrifice of capital that might otherwise benefit successors.

National Savings and Investments (NS&I)

NS&I is one of the biggest savings institutions in the country. It is guaranteed by the government and all investments are backed by HM Treasury. It is extremely easy to invest in NS&I products, as all you need do is go to the Post Office for information or telephone the NS&I Customer Enquiries on Tel: 0845 964 5000, all calls are charged at local rates. Their website is www.nsandi.com.

Most types of investment offered by NS&I are broadly similar to those provided by banks and other financial bodies. NS&I Savings Certificates, of which there are two types – Fixed Interest and Inflation-beating – are free of tax. Although in most cases they do not pay a particularly high rate of interest, any investment that is tax-free is of potential interest, especially to higher-rate taxpayers. A long-standing feature of NS&I has been that non-taxpayers enjoyed the benefit of income receipts being paid gross, without deduction of tax. The one advantage that NS&I still offers non-taxpayers is that there is no need for them to complete an HM Revenue & Customs form to receive their money in full, as this is automatic.

The main investments offered by National Savings and Investments are:

▨ **Easy Access Savings Account.** This is an easy way to build up your savings, with instant access to your money and the option to save regularly by standing order. You can invest between £100 and £2 million. The account offers variable, tiered rates of interest and allows instant access through the Post Office or cash machines.

▨ **Income bonds.** Suitable if you are interested in earning monthly income and have easy access to your money. These pay fairly attractive variable, tiered rates of interest, increasing with larger investments. Interest is taxable, but paid in full without deduction of tax at source. You can invest between £500 and £1 million. There is no set term for the investment.

Fixed Interest Savings Certificates. These will earn you guaranteed and tax-free returns. Offers a moderate rate of interest. You can invest from £100 to £15,000 per issue. For maximum benefit, you must hold the certificates for five years.

Inflation-beating Savings Certificates. If you want to make sure your investment grows ahead of inflation, tax-free. You can invest from £100 to £15,000 per issue. There is a fixed rate of interest, index-linking to the Retail Prices Index. No index-linking or interest will be earned on Certificates cahsed in within one year of purchase. Certificates must be retained for either three or five years. Interest is tax free.

Children's Bonus Bonds. If you want to give a child a long-term tax-free investment. Bonds are sold in multiples of £25 and the maximum purchase per child is £3,000. Investment term is five years at a time until 21st birthday. Interest rates fixed for five years at a time plus guaranteed bonus. These are tax-free for parents and children and need not be declared to HM Revenue & Customs.

Guaranteed Income Bonds. If you want a monthly income with the certainty of knowing exactly what return you will get on your money without touching your capital investment. The income, which is paid monthly, is taxable and paid net. Minimum purchase is £500; the maximum, £1 million. Choice of terms – currently 1, 3 and 5 years. Interest rates guaranteed for length of chosen term.

▓ **Guaranteed Growth Bonds.** These give a guaranteed return on your investment, and offer a choice of fixed-rate terms. If you want to invest for a set term with the certainty of knowing exactly what return you will get on your money. Minimum purchase is £500; the maximum, £1 million. Choice of terms – currently 1, 3 and 5 years. Interest rates guaranteed for the length of term chosen. Interest is taxable and paid net.

NS&I also offers cash ISAs a direct ISA, Guaranteed Equity Bonds, an Investment Account and of course Premium Bonds, of which you can now hold up to £30,000 worth.

Complaints. Disputes should be referred to the Director of Savings. If you are not satisfied with the service given here, your complaint can be referred to the Financial Ombudsman Service: Tel: 0845 080 1800; email: complaint.info@finan cial-ombudsman.org.uk; website: www.financial-ombuds man.org.uk.

Variable-interest accounts

Few people who rely on interest from their savings to provide them with extra income in their retirement will need reminding that interest rates go down as well as up. Over the past few years, most banks and building societies have introduced interest-bearing current accounts. These are not a suitable place for anyone to keep large savings for more than a short time. If you are tempted to switch to an interest-bearing current account, you should check very carefully what charges apply if you dip into overdraft.

A point to investigate is whether there is a fixed monthly or other charge. This can sometimes change at fairly short notice. You should check your monthly statement carefully and consider moving your account if you are dissatisfied. Banks and building societies frequently introduce new accounts with introductory bonuses, which are then slashed in value after a few months. Although this could equally apply to internet accounts, they could still be worth investigating as, generally speaking, they tend to offer more competitive rates.

Although keeping track may be fairly time-consuming, at least comparing the rates offered by different savings institutions has become very much easier, as all advertisements for savings products must now quote the annual equivalent rate (AER). Unlike the former variety of ways of expressing interest rates, the AER provides a true comparison taking into account the frequency of interest payments and whether or not interest is compounded.

Definition. Other than the interest-bearing current accounts described above, these are all savings accounts of one form or another, arranged with banks, building societies, the National Savings and Investments Bank and with some financial institutions that operate such accounts jointly with banks. They include: instant access accounts, high-interest accounts and fixed-term savings accounts.

Your money collects interest, which may be automatically credited to your account or for which you may receive a regular cheque. Some institutions pay interest annually, others – on some or all of their accounts – will pay it monthly. If you have a preference, this is a point to check.

Although you may get a poor return on your money when interest rates drop, your savings will nearly always be safe as you are not taking any kind of investment risk. Moreover, provided you deal with an authorised bank, up to £50,000 of your money will be 100 per cent protected under the Financial Services Compensation Scheme. These changes were announced in October 2008.

Access. Access to your money depends on the type of account you choose: you may have an ATM card and/or chequebook and withdraw your money when you want; you may have to give a week's notice or slightly longer; or if you enter into a term account, you will have to leave your money deposited for the agreed specified period. In general, accounts where a slightly longer period of notice is required earn a better rate of interest.

Sum deposited. You can open a savings account with as little as £1. For certain types of account, the minimum investment could be anything from £500 to about £5,000. The terms tend to vary according to how keen the institutions are, at a given time, to attract small investors.

Tax. With the exception of cash ISAs, which are tax-free, and of the National Savings and Investments Bank, where interest is paid gross, tax is deducted at source – so you can spend the money without worrying about the tax implications. However, you must enter the interest on your tax return; and if you are a higher-rate taxpayer, you will of course have additional liability.

Basic-rate taxpayers pay 20 per cent on their bank and building society interest. Higher-rate taxpayers pay 40 per cent. Non-taxpayers can arrange to have their interest paid in full by completing a certificate (R85 available from the HMRC or their bank) that enables the financial institution to pay the interest gross. If you largely rely on your savings income and believe you are or have been paying excess tax you can reclaim this from HM Revenue & Customs.

NB: There has been some rather disturbing news recently about Cash ISA savers being badly let down by banks and building societies when they try to transfer their accounts. Because of poor administration in some cases they have not had access to their money for months. ISA rules prevent savers from switching their money between accounts themselves, because that would lose them the tax-free benefit. The trap is caused by a ten-year-old system in which ISA providers write each other cheques to move the money rather than using faster electronic transfers. Under the system the provider holding your money has a month after receiving your transfer request to move your cash. If you are likely to be transferring your savings from one account to another, keep an eye on this potential hazard.

Choosing a savings account

There are two main areas of choice: the type of savings account and where to invest your money. The relative attractions of the different types of account and of the institutions themselves can vary, according to the terms being offered at the time. Generally speaking, however, the basic points are as follows.

instant access savings account. This attracts a relatively low rate of interest. But it is both easy to set up and very flexible, as you can add small or large savings when you like and can usually withdraw your money without any notice. It is a much better option than simply leaving your money in a current account and is an excellent temporary home for your cash if you are saving short term for, say, a holiday. However, it is not recommended as a long-term savings plan.

High-interest savings account. Your money earns a higher rate of interest than it would in an ordinary savings account. However, to open a high-interest account you will need to deposit a minimum sum, which could be £500 to £1,000. Although you can always add to this amount, if your balance drops below the required minimum, your money will immediately stop earning the higher interest rate. The terms often vary between one institution and another. There may be a minimum and/or maximum monthly sum you can pay into the account. Also, some accounts have a fixed term, at the end of which your money would no longer earn the more favourable rate of interest.

Fixed-term savings account. You deposit your money for an agreed period of time, which can vary from a few months to over a year. In return for this commitment, you will normally be paid a superior rate of interest. As with high-interest accounts, there is a minimum investment: roughly £1,500 to £10,000. If you need to withdraw your money before the end of the agreed term, there are usually hefty penalties. Before entering into a term account, you need to be sure that you can afford to leave the money in the account. Additionally, you will need to take a view about interest rates: if they are generally low, your money may be better invested elsewhere.

Equity-linked savings account. Offers a potentially better rate of return, as the interest is calculated in line with the growth in the stock market. Should the market fall, you may lose the interest but your capital should normally remain protected. The minimum investment varies from about £500 to £5,000 and, depending on the institution, the money may need to remain deposited for perhaps as much as five years. As with any investment, it is important to ensure that you fully understand all the terms and conditions – and if anything is unclear, that you ask to have the point explained to you properly in simple language.

ISA savings. With an ISA you are allowed to save up to £7,200 each year and not pay UK tax on the income you receive from your investment. An ISA can be made up of an investment in cash, or investments such as stocks and shares or insurance. You can invest in two separate ISAs in any one tax year; one cash ISA and one stocks and shares ISA. For cash ISAs, the limit is £3,600 a year, and must be with one provider in any one tax year. For stocks and shares ISAs, you can invest up to £7,200 a year, with one provider in any one tax year. If you want both a cash ISA and a stocks and shares ISA in the same tax year, the separate limits for each type of ISA still apply, but the limit cannot exceed £7,200. The ISAs can be either with the same or with different providers.

Information. For banks, enquire direct at your nearest high street branch. There will be leaflets available, describing the different accounts in detail. Or if you have any questions, you can ask to see your bank manager. You can also investigate the other banks to see whether they offer better terms. For building societies, enquire at any building society branch. There is such a wide range of these that it is advisable to look at a number of them as the terms and conditions may vary quite widely.

The **Building Societies Association** offers a free range of helpful leaflets and information sheets, including: *Lost Savings? – Taxation of Building Society Interest*; *Individual Savings Accounts and Building Societies*; and *The Child Trust Fund*. A list of members, giving head office addresses and telephone numbers, is also available. All leaflets can be ordered by calling the Consumer Helpline on Tel: 020 7520 5900; or by email: information@bsa.org.uk; website: www.bsa.org.uk.

The safety of your investment. Investors are protected by the legislative framework in which societies operate, and in common with bank customers, their money (up to a maximum of £50,000) is protected under the **Financial Services Compensation Scheme** (FSCS). Further details about the scheme are available from the FSCS: Tel: 020 7892 7300; email: enquiries@fscs.org.uk; website: www. fscs.org.uk.

Complaints. If you have a complaint against a bank or building society, you can appeal to the **Financial Ombudsman Service (FOS)** to investigate the matter, provided the complaint has already been taken through the particular institution's own internal disputes procedure. The FOS details are provided on page 99.

Fixed-interest securities

In contrast to variable-interest accounts, fixed-interest securities offer a fixed rate of interest, which you are paid regardless of what happens to interest rates generally. If you buy when the fixed rate is high and interest rates fall, you will nevertheless continue to be paid interest at the high rate specified in the contract note. However, if interest rates rise above the level when you bought, you will not benefit from the increase. Generally these securities give high income but only modest, if any, capital appreciation. The list includes high-interest gilts, permanent interest-bearing shares, local authority bonds and stock exchange loans, debentures and preference shares.

Gilt-edged securities

Definition. Usually known as 'gilts', these are stocks issued by the government, which guarantees both the interest payable and the repayment price, which is promised on a given date. The maturity date varies and can be anything from a few months to 20 years or longer. Accordingly, stocks are variously known as: short-dated, medium-dated and long-dated. A further category is undated. Additionally, there are index-linked gilts. Prices for gilts are quoted per £100 of nominal stock. For example, a stock may be quoted as 10 per cent Treasury Stock 2010, 99½ – 100¼. In plain English, this means the following:

▓ 10 per cent represents the interest you will be paid. The rate is fixed and will not vary, whatever happens to interest rates generally. You will receive the interest payment twice yearly, 5 per cent each time.

▨ You are buying Treasury Stock.

▨ The maturity date is 2010.

▨ To buy the stock, you will have to pay £100.25p (ie 100 ¼).

▨ If you want to sell the stock, the market price you will get is £99.50p (ie 99½).

In addition, when buying or selling, regard has to be given to the accrued interest that will have to be added to or subtracted from the price quoted. Gilts are complicated by the fact that you can either retain them until their maturity date, in which case the government will return the capital in full, or you can sell them on the London Stock Exchange at market value.

Index-linked gilts, although operating on the same broad principle, are different in effect. They are designed to shield investors against inflation; they pay very low interest but are redeemable at a higher price than the initial purchase price, as their value is geared to the cost of living. They are most valuable when inflation is high but are even more sensitive than other gilts to optimum timing when buying or selling.

Tax. Gilt interest from whatever source is paid gross. Gross payment does not mean that you avoid paying tax, simply that you must allow for a future tax bill before spending the money. Recipients who prefer to receive the money net of tax can request for this to be arranged. A particular attraction of gilts is that no capital gains tax is charged on any profit you may have made. But equally no relief is allowed for loss.

How to buy. You can buy gilts through banks, building societies, a stockbroker or financial intermediary. Or you can purchase them through Computershare Investor Services. In all cases, you will be charged commission. Prices of gilts are published every day in all the quality newspapers under the heading 'British Funds'. You may also find it helpful to refer to the section headed 'Bonds'.

Assessment. Gilts normally pay reasonably good interest and offer excellent security, in that they are backed by the government. You can sell at very short notice and the stock is normally accepted by banks as security for loans, if you want to run an overdraft. Index-linked gilts, which overcome the inflation problem, are generally speaking a better investment for higher-rate taxpayers – not least because the interest paid is very low.

Gilt plans. This is a technique for linking the purchase of gilt-edged securities and with-profit life insurance policies to provide security of capital and income over a 10- to 20-year period. It is a popular investment for the commuted lump sum taken on retirement. These plans are normally obtainable from financial intermediaries, who should be authorised by the FSA.

Permanent interest-bearing shares (PIBS)

These are a form of investment offered by some building

societies to financial institutions and private investors, as a means of raising share capital. They have several features in common with gilts, as follows. They pay a fixed rate of interest that is set at the date of issue: this is likely to be on the high side when interest rates generally are low and on the low side when interest rates are high. The interest is usually paid twice yearly and – again, similar to gilts – there is no stamp duty to pay, nor capital gains tax on profits. Despite the fact that PIBS are issued by building societies, they are very different from normal building society investments and have generally been rated as being in the medium- to high-risk category. Anyone thinking of investing their money should seek professional advice. To buy the shares, you would need to go to a stockbroker or financial adviser.

Equities

These are all stocks and shares, purchased in different ways and involving varying degrees of risk. They are designed to achieve capital appreciation as well as give you some regular income. Most allow you to get your money out within a week. In the past, equities were by and large only considered suitable for a privileged minority, but recently the number of shareholders is estimated to have soared to well over 15 million people. One reason is that equities can be excellent money-spinners. Another is that over the last few years, investment has become very much easier, largely as a result of the increase in the number of internet and telephone share-dealing facilities.

As many will know to their cost from the recent market volatility, equities are always risky. But for those who believe in caution, the gamble can be substantially reduced by avoiding obviously speculative investments and by choosing a spread of investments, rather than putting all your eggs in one basket. Equities include ordinary shares, unit trusts, OEICs (see below), investment trusts and REITs (see page 65).

Unit trusts and OEICs

Definition. Unit trusts and OEICs (open-ended investment companies, a modern equivalent of unit trusts) offer the opportunity of investing collectively in a range of assets with other investors. Your money is pooled in a fund run by professional managers, who invest the capital in a wide range of assets, including equities, bonds and cash. The advantages are that it is usually less risky than buying individual shares, it is simple to understand, you get professional management and there are no day-to-day decisions to make. Additionally, every fund is required by law to have a trustee (called a depository in the case of OEICs) to protect investors' interests.

The minimum investment in some of the more popular funds can be as little as £25; in others, it can be as high as £10,000. There is often a front-end fee, and sometimes an exit fee, which varies from group to group and fund to fund. Investors' contributions to the fund are divided into units (shares in OEICs) in proportion to the amount they have invested. As with ordinary shares, you can sell all or some of your investment by telling the fund manager that you wish to do so. The price you will receive is called 'the bid price'. The price at which you buy a unit is called 'the offer price'.

How to obtain. Units and shares can be purchased from banks, building societies, insurance companies, stock-brokers, specialist investment fund providers, independent financial advisers, directly from the management group and via the internet. You may be asked to complete a form – stating how much you want to invest in which particular fund – and then return it to the company with your cheque. Alternatively, you may be able to deal over the telephone or internet.

For a list of unit trusts and OEICs, you can look in the *Financial Times*. You can also contact **Investment FactLine** Information Service on Tel: 020 7269 4639 (website: www.investmentuk.org./investors) to obtain a guide to investing called *Introducing Investment*, as well as various factsheets on such topics as ISAs, ethical investment, unit trusts and tax. Tables comparing the performance of the various funds are published in specialist magazines or on websites such as *Money Management*, *Money Observer* and *What Investment*. With over 2,000 funds from which to choose, it is important to get independent professional advice. For further information see Independent financial advisers, Chapter 3.

Tax. Units and shares invested through an ISA have special advantages (see Individual Savings Account, page 67). Otherwise, tax treatment is identical to ordinary shares (see Tax, page 66).

Assessment. An ideal method for smaller investors to buy stocks and shares: both less risky and easier. This applies especially to tracker funds, which have the added advantage that charges are normally very low. Some of the more specialist funds are also suitable for those with a significant investment portfolio.

Complaints. Complaints about unit trusts and OEICs are handled by the **Financial Ombudsman Service (FOS)**. It has power to order awards of up to £100,000. Before approaching the FOS, you must first try to resolve the problem with the management company direct via their internal complaints procedure. Details of the FOS are provided on page 99.

Ordinary shares listed on the London Stock Exchange

Definition. Public companies issue shares as a way of raising money. When you buy shares and become a shareholder in a company, you own a small part of the business and are entitled to participate in its profits through a dividend, which is normally paid six-monthly. Dividends go up and down according to how well the company is doing and it is possible that in a bad year no dividends at all will be paid. However, in good years, dividends can increase very substantially.

The money you invest is unsecured. This means that, quite apart from any dividends, your capital could be reduced in value – or if the company goes bankrupt, you could lose the lot. Against this, if the company performs well, you could substantially increase your wealth. The value of a company's shares is decided by the stock market. The price of a share can fluctuate daily, and this will affect both how much you have to pay if you want to buy and how much you will make (or lose) if you want to sell. You could visit the London Stock Exchange website (www.londonstockexchange.com) to find a list of brokers in your area who would be willing to deal for you. Alternatively, you could go to the securities department of your bank – or to one of the authorised share shops – which would place the order for you.

Whether you use a stockbroker, a share shop, a telephone share-dealing service or the internet, you will be charged both commission and stamp duty, which is currently 0.5 per cent. Unless you use a nominee account (see below), you will be issued with a share certificate that you or your financial adviser must keep, as you will have to produce it when you wish to sell all or part of your holding. It is likely, when approaching a stockbroker or other share-dealing service, that you will be asked to deposit money for your investment upfront or advised that you should use a nominee account. This is because of the introduction of several new systems, designed to speed up – and streamline – the share-dealing process.

There are three types of share, all quoted on the London Stock Exchange, that are potentially suitable for small investors. These are investment companies, REITs and convertible loan stocks. Other possibilities, but only for those who can afford more risky investments, are warrants and zero coupon loan stocks.

Investment companies are companies that invest in the shares of other companies. They pool investors' money, and so enable those with quite small amounts to spread the risk by gaining exposure to a wide portfolio of shares, run by a professional fund manager. There are over 300 different companies from which to choose. For a range of factsheets on investment companies, contact **The Association of Investment Companies**: Tel: 020 7282 5555; email: enquiries@theaic.co.uk; website: www.theaic.co.uk.

Real estate investment trusts (REITs). These are a fairly new type of fund, quoted on the London Stock Exchange, that, operating similarly to investment trusts, pool investors' money and invest it for them collectively in commercial and residential property. They offer individuals a cheap, simple and potentially less risky way of buying shares in a spread of properties, with the added attraction that the funds themselves are more tax-efficient, as both rental income and profits from sales are tax-free within the fund. Also, if wanted, they can be held within an ISA or Self-Invested Personal Pension. There are numerous UK companies who have converted to REIT status. Stockbrokers and independent financial advisers are able to provide information and it is recommended that professional advice is taken before investing.

Convertible loan stocks give you a fixed guaranteed income for a certain length of time and offer you the opportunity to convert them into ordinary shares. Although capital appreciation prospects are lower, the advantage of convertible loans is that they usually provide significantly higher income than ordinary dividends. They are also allowable for ISAs.

Zero coupon loan stocks. These stocks provide no income during their life but pay an enhanced capital sum on matur-ity. They would normally only be recommended for higher-rate taxpayers and professional advice is strongly recommended.

Warrants are issued by companies or investment trusts to existing shareholders either at launch or by way of an additional bonus. Each warrant carries the right of the shareholder to purchase additional shares at a predetermined price on specific dates in the future. As such, warrants will command their own price on the stock market. These are a high-risk investment and professional advice is essential.

Tax. All UK shares pay dividends net of 10 per cent corporation tax. Basic-rate and non-taxpayers have no further liability to income tax. Higher-rate taxpayers must pay further income tax at 22.5 per cent. Quite apart from income tax, if during the year you make profits by selling shares that in total exceed £9,200, you would be liable for capital gains tax. **NB:** from April 2008 CGT is calculated at the flat rate of 18 per cent.

Assessment. Although dividend payments generally start low, in good companies they are likely to increase over the years and so provide a first-class hedge against inflation. The best equities are an excellent investment. In others, you can lose all your money. Good advice is critical as this is a high-risk/high-reward market.

Individual Savings Account (ISA)

Definition. ISAs are the savings accounts that the government launched in April 1999 as a replacement for PEPs and TESSAs. They contain many of the same advantages in that all income and gains generated in the account are tax free.

There is a subscription limit. There are two types of ISA: cash ISAs and stocks and shares ISAs.

2008 changes. The annual subscription limit was increased in April 2008 from £7,000 to £7,200, making it possible to invest a maximum of up to £3,600 in a cash ISA plus a further £3,600 in a stocks and shares ISA. Alternatively, you can now invest up to £7,200 in a stocks and shares ISA. Importantly, the distinction between mini- and maxi-ISAs was removed, with the advantage that cash savings accounts are now transferable into stocks and shares ISAs.

Tax. ISAs are completely free of all income tax and capital gains tax. However, as you may remember, the 10 per cent dividend tax credit was scrapped in April 2004. Also, you should be aware that a 20 per cent charge is levied on all interest accruing from non-invested money held in an ISA that is not specifically a cash ISA.

Assessment. ISAs offer a simple, flexible way of starting, or improving, a savings plan, although sadly they are no longer as attractive as they once were. Although cash ISAs remain useful, as all interest is tax free, stocks and shares ISAs – although still potentially worthwhile for higher-rate taxpayers – offer fewer advantages to basic-rate taxpayers as a result of the charges and the removal of the dividend tax credit.

Child Trust Funds

Child Trust Funds are designed to start every baby off with a savings plan to mature at the time of his/her 18th birthday.

Although clearly of no direct benefit to readers, they could be of interest to grandparents who would like to help grandchildren build up a nest egg for the future. All children born since 1 September 2002 receive a voucher worth £250 to be invested in a fund until they reach 18. Children of less wealthy families are given £500. A further payment of £250/£500 will be added at age seven. Family and friends are allowed to contribute up to a maximum of £1,200 a year into the fund. The money can be invested in cash, shares, bonds plus most FSA-approved schemes and all growth in the fund is tax free. It can then be rolled into ISAs once the child becomes 18. If the money is not invested after a year of receipt of the voucher, the money will be invested in a special 'stakeholder account'. There is no need to claim as vouchers are sent automatically to everyone receiving child benefit.

Long-term lock-ups

Certain types of investment, mostly offered by insurance companies, provide fairly high guaranteed growth in exchange for your undertaking to leave a lump sum with them or to pay regular premiums for a fixed period, usually five years or longer. The list includes: life assurance policies, investment bonds and some types of National Savings certificates.

Life assurance policies

Definition. Life assurance can provide you with one of two main benefits: it can either provide your successors with money when you die or it can be used as a savings plan to provide you with a lump sum (or income) on a fixed date. In recent years, however, both types of scheme have become more flexible and many policies allow you to incorporate features of the other. This can have great advantages but the result is that some of the definitions appear a bit contradictory. There are three basic types of life assurance: whole life policies, term policies and endowment policies.

Whole life policies are designed to pay out on your death. In its most straightforward form, the scheme works as follows: you pay a premium every year and, when you die, your beneficiaries receive the money. As with an ordinary household policy, the insurance only holds good if you continue the payments. If one year you did not pay and were to die, the policy could be void and your successors would receive nothing.

Term policies involve a definite commitment. As opposed to paying premiums every year, you elect to make regular payments for an agreed period: for example, until such time as your children have completed their education, say eight years. If you die during this period, your family will be paid the agreed sum in full. If you die after the end of the term (when you have stopped making payments), your family will normally receive nothing.

Endowment policies are essentially savings plans. You sign a contract to pay regular premiums over a number of years and in exchange receive a lump sum on a specific date. Most endowment policies are written for periods varying from 10 to 25 years. Once you have committed yourself, you have to go on paying every year (as with term assurance). There are heavy penalties if, after having paid for a number of years, you decide that you no longer wish to continue.

An important feature of endowment policies is that they are linked in with death cover. If you die before the policy matures, the remaining payments are excused and your successors will be paid a lump sum on your death. The amount of money you stand to receive, however, can vary hugely, depending on the charges and how generous a bonus the insurance company feels it can afford on the policy's maturity. Over the past few years, pay-outs have been considerably lower than their earlier projections might have suggested.

Options. Both whole life policies and endowment policies offer two basic options: with profits or without profits. Very briefly the difference is as follows.

Without profits. This is sometimes known as 'guaranteed sum assured'. What it means is that the insurance company guarantees you a specific fixed sum (provided of course you meet the various terms and conditions). You know the amount in advance and this is the sum you – or your successors – will be paid.

With profits. You are paid a guaranteed fixed sum plus an addition, based on the profits that the insurance company has made by investing your annual or monthly payments. The basic premiums are higher and, by definition, the profits element is not known in advance. If the insurance company has invested your money wisely, a 'with profits' policy provides a useful hedge against inflation. If its investment policy is mediocre, you could have paid higher premiums for very little extra return.

Unit linked. This is a refinement of the 'with profits' policy, in that the investment element of the policy is linked in with a unit trust.

Other basics. Premiums can normally be paid monthly or annually, as you prefer. Size of premium varies enormously, depending on the type of policy you choose and the amount of cover you want. Also, of course, some insurance companies are more competitive than others. As very general guidance, £50–75 a month would probably be a normal starting figure. Again as a generalisation, higher premiums tend to give better value as relatively less of your contribution is swallowed up in administrative costs.

As a condition of insuring you, some policies require that you have a medical check. This is more likely to apply if very large sums are involved. More usually, all that is required is that you fill in and sign a declaration of health. It is very important that this should be completed honestly: if you make a claim on your policy and it is subsequently discovered that you gave misleading information, your policy could be declared void and the insurance company could refuse to pay.

Many insurance companies offer a better deal if you are a non-smoker. Some also offer more generous terms if you are teetotal. Women generally pay less than men of the same age because of their longer life expectancy.

How to obtain. Policies are usually available through banks, insurance companies, independent financial advisers (IFAs) and building societies. The biggest problem for most people is the sheer volume of choice. Another difficulty can be understanding the small print: terms and conditions that sound very similar may obscure important differences that could affect your benefit. An accountant could advise you in general terms whether you are being offered a good deal or otherwise. However, if it is a question of choosing a specific policy best suited to your requirements, it is usually advisable to consult an IFA. For help in finding an IFA in your area, contact **IFA Promotion Ltd**: Tel: 0800 085 3250; email: contact@ifap.org.uk; website: www.unbiased. co.uk.

Disclosure rules. Advisers selling financial products have to abide by a set of disclosure rules, requiring them to give clients certain essential information before a contract is signed. Although for a number of years the requirements have included the provision of both a 'key features' document (explaining the product, the risk factors, charges, benefits, surrender value if the policy is terminated early, tax treatment and salesperson's commission/remuneration) and a 'suitability letter', explaining why a particular product/policy was recommended, the FSA recently decided to revamp the rules in order to provide consumers with clearer and more comprehensive information.

As a result, advisers must now give potential clients two 'key facts' documents: one, entitled *About our Services*, describing the range of services and the type of advice on offer; and the second entitled *About the Cost of our Services*, including details of their own commission charges and – for comparison purposes – the average market rate. Importantly too, independent financial advisers (IFAs) must offer clients the choice of paying fees or paying by commission.

The **Association of British Insurers (ABI)** has a number of useful information sheets on life insurance. Contact ABI: Tel: 020 7600 3333; email: info@abi.org.uk; website: www.abi.org.uk.

Tax. Under current legislation, the proceeds of a qualifying policy – whether taken as a lump sum or in regular income payments (as in the case of Family Income Benefit) – are free of all tax. If, as applies to many people, you have a life insurance policy written into a trust, there is a possibility that it could be hit by the new inheritance tax rules affecting trusts if the sum it is expected to pay out is above the (2008/09) £312,000 IHT threshold. Best advice is to check with a solicitor.

Assessment. Life assurance is normally a sensible investment, whether the aim is to provide death cover or the benefits of a lump sum to boost your retirement income. It has the merit of being very attractive from a tax angle and additionally certain policies provide good capital appreciation – although a point to be aware of is that recent bonuses have tended to be considerably lower than their projected amount. However, you are locked into a long-term commitment, so, even more than in most areas, choosing the right policy is very important.

Complaints. Complaints about life assurance products, including alleged mis-selling, are handled by the **Financial Ombudsman Service (FOS)**, details provided on page 99. Before approaching the FOS, you would first need to try to resolve a dispute with the company direct.

Alternatives to surrendering a policy. As already mentioned, there are heavy penalties if you surrender an endowment policy before its maturity. Some people, however, either because they can no longer afford the payments or for some other reason, wish to terminate the agreement – regardless of any losses they may make/or investment gains they sacrifice. Instead of simply surrendering the policy to the insurance company, people in this situation may be able to sell the policy for a sum that is higher than its surrender value. As a first step, you might usefully contact the **Association of Policy Market Makers**: Tel: 0845 011 9406; email: valuations@apmm.org; website www.apmm.org, who can put you in contact with a number of suitable firms.

For those looking for investment possibilities, second-hand policies could be worth investigating. Known as traded endowment policies (TEPs), they offer the combination of a low-risk investment with a good potential return. Owing to increased supply, there is currently a wide range of individual policies and a number of specialist funds managed by financial institutions. A full list of appropriate financial institutions and authorised dealers that buy and sell mid-term policies is obtainable from the **Association of Policy Market Makers**. They can also arrange for suitable policies to be valued by member firms, free of charge.

Bonds

You may have read that as you near retirement you should increasingly be moving your investments from equities into bonds. The reason for this advice is that although bonds generally offer less opportunity for capital growth, they tend to be lower risk as they are less exposed to stock market volatility and also have the advantage of producing a regular guaranteed income. Although normally recommended as sensible, a particular problem owing to the recent downturn in the stock market is that you could make a loss by selling some of your shares now, whereas possibly if you wait, they might recover. A bigger problem is that there are different types of bonds, with varying degrees of risk, which it is important you should understand.

The three main types are: government bonds – called gilt-edged securities or 'gilts' – corporate bonds and investment bonds. Gilts are the least risky as they are secured by the government, which guarantees both the interest payable and the return of your capital in full if you hold the stocks until their maturity. Corporate bonds are fairly similar except that, as opposed to loaning your money to the government, you are lending it to a large company or taking out a deben-ture. The risk is higher because, although you would normally only be recommended to buy a corporate bond from a highly rated company, there is always the possibility that the company could fail and might not be able to make the payments promised. In general, the higher the guaran-teed interest payments, the less totally secure the company in question.

Although gilts and corporate bonds are normally recom-mended for cautious investors, investment bonds (described below) are different in that they offer potentially much higher rewards but also carry a much higher degree of risk. Because even gilts can be influenced by timing and other factors, if you are thinking of buying bonds expert advice is very strongly recommended.

Investment bonds

Definition. This is the method of investing a lump sum with an insurance company in the hope of receiving a much larger sum back at a specific date – normally a few years later. All bonds offer life assurance cover as part of the deal. A particular feature of some bonds is that the managers have wide discretion to invest your money in almost any type of security. The risk/reward ratio is, therefore, very high.

Although bonds can achieve significant capital appreciation, you can also lose a high percentage of your investment. An exception is guaranteed equity bonds, which, although linked to the performance of the FTSE 100 or other stock market index, will protect your capital if shares fall. However, although your capital should be returned in full at the end of the fixed term (usually five years), a point not always appreciated is that, should markets fall, far from making any return on your investment you will have lost money in real terms: first, because your capital will have fallen in value, once inflation is taken into account; second, because you will have lost out on any interest that your money could have earned had it been on deposit.

All bond proceeds are free of basic-rate tax but higher-rate tax is payable. However, the higher-rate taxpayer can withdraw up to 5 per cent of his/her initial investment each year and defer the higher-rate tax liability for 20 years or until the bond is cashed in full – whichever is earlier. Although there is no capital gains tax on redemption of a bond (or on switching between funds), some corporation tax may be payable by the fund itself, which could affect its investment performance. Companies normally charge a front-end fee of around 5 per cent plus a small annual management fee, usually not related to performance.

Tax. Tax treatment is very complicated, as it is influenced by your marginal income tax rate in the year of encashment. For this reason, it is generally best to buy a bond when you are working and plan to cash it after retirement. **NB**: If you hold a policy with personal portfolio bonds, you should speak to your financial adviser or insurance company as there have been some recent changes to the tax regulations. It appears likely that despite the new 18 per cent CGT rate applicable since April 2008, some higher-rate tax-payers could still be hit by the (old) 40 per cent tax. They would be strongly advised to check their policy with an accountant.

Assessment. This investment is more likely to be attractive to the sophisticated investor with high earnings in the years before retirement.

Useful reading

Fair Shares by Simon Rose. A layman's guide to buying and selling stocks and shares. Mercury. Price £12.99.

Investor protection

Over the past few years, great strides have been made regarding investor protection. There is now a set of stringent rules on businesses offering investment services and also a powerful regulatory body, the Financial Services Authority (FSA), which is charged by parliament with responsibility for ensuring that firms are 'fit and proper' to operate in the investment field and for monitoring their activities on an ongoing basis.

The main effects of these safeguards are as follows:

▨ Investment businesses (including accountants or solicitors giving investment advice) are not at liberty to operate without authorisation or exemption from the FSA. Operating without such authorisation (or exemption) is a criminal offence.

▨ Previously, under what was known as polarisation, businesses providing advice on investment products could either operate as 'tied agents', limited to selling their own in-house products (or those of a single provider) or had to be independent financial advisers, advising on products across the whole market. The FSA recently took the view that this was too restrictive and, with the aim of providing consumers with greater choice, has now authorised a new category of adviser known as a 'multi-tied agent', able to offer the products from a chosen panel of providers.

▨ Whether tied, multi-tied or independent, advisers must give customers certain information before a contract is signed. Under the disclosure rules, which were revised in 2005, this includes two 'key facts' documents – *About our Services* and *About the Cost of our Services* – plus a 'suitability' letter explaining the rationale on which recommendations are based.

▦ Among other important detail, the information must provide a breakdown of the charges (expressed in cash terms), describe the payment options (commission and/or fee) and, in the case of commission, must quote both the adviser's own commission and the average market rate.

▦ Investment businesses must adhere to a proper complaints procedure with provision for customers to receive fair redress, where appropriate.

▦ Unsolicited visits and telephone calls to sell investments are for the most part banned. Where these are allowed for package products (such as unit trusts and life assurance), should a sale result the customer will have a 14-day 'cooling-off period' (or a seven-day 'right to withdraw' period if the packaged product is held within an ISA and the sale follows advice from the firm). The cooling-off period is to give the customer time to explore other options before deciding whether to cancel the contract or not.

A single regulatory authority

As a result of the Financial Services Markets Act 2000, all the former self-regulating organisations (including the PIA,

IMRO and SFA) have now been merged under the Financial Services Authority (FSA) with the purpose of improving investor protection and of providing a single contact point for enquiries. Should you need to contact the **Financial Services Authority**: Tel: 0845 606 1234; website: www.fsa. gov.uk.

A single Ombudsman scheme

Since December 2001 there has also been a single statutory Financial Ombudsman Service (FOS). A welcome result of there being a single Ombudsman scheme is that the FOS covers complaints across almost the entire range of financial services and products – from banking services, endowment mortgages and personal pensions to household insurance and stocks and shares. The list also includes unit trusts and OEICs, life assurance, FSAVCs and equity release schemes. A further advantage is that the FOS applies a single set of rules to all complaints. The FOS now covers the consumer-credit activities of businesses with a consumer-credit licence issued by the Office of Fair Trading; these include debt consolidation, consumer hire, debt collecting and pawnbrokers.

Complaints

If you have a complaint against an authorised firm, in the first instance you should take it up with the firm concerned: you may be able to resolve the matter at this level, since all authorised firms are obliged to have a proper complaints-handling procedure.

The **Financial Ombudsman Service** (see details on page 99) advises that the best approach is to start by contacting the person you originally dealt with and, if you phone, to keep a written note of all telephone calls. If complaining by letter, it helps to set out the facts in logical order, to stick to what is relevant and to include important details such as customer, policy and account number. You should also keep a copy of all letters, both for your own record purposes and also as useful evidence should you need to take the matter further.

Warning

The existence of the FSA enables you to check on the credentials of anyone purporting to be a financial adviser or trying to persuade you to invest your money in an insurance policy, bond, unit or investment trust, equity, futures contract or similar. However, if either they or the organisation they represent are not authorised by the FSA, you are very strongly recommended to leave well alone. You can check whether a firm is authorised by ringing the FSA's Central Register on: Tel: 0845 606 1234; website: www.fsa.gov.uk.

Useful reading

Choosing a Financial Adviser – How keyfacts can help you and *Capital-at-risk products* (products where you could lose some of the money you invest); available free from the Financial Services Authority (FSA): Tel: 0845 606 1234; website: www.fsa.gov.uk.

3

Independent financial advisers: IFAs

If there is one golden rule when it comes to money matters, it must be: if in doubt, ask. Although most professional advisers are extremely sound, not everyone who proffers advice is qualified to do so. Checking credentials has become much easier under the Financial Services Act.

Before making contact with a financial advisor it is generally a good idea to try to sort out your priorities. One reason for doing some pre-planning is that certain types of advisers – for example, insurance brokers – do not specifically charge you for their time. Other professional advisers, such as accountants and solicitors, charge their fees by the hour.

Choosing an adviser

When choosing an adviser, there are usually four main considerations: respectability, suitability, price and convenience. Where your money is concerned, you cannot afford to take unnecessary risks. Establishing that an individual is a member of a recognised institution is a basic safeguard. If you are thinking of using a particular adviser you should certainly check on their reputation, ask for references from some of their existing clients. Most reputable professionals will be delighted to assist, as it means that the relationship will be founded on a basis of greater trust and confidence.

Accountants

Accountants are specialists in matters concerning taxation. If there is scope to do so, they can advise on ways of reducing your tax liability and can assess the various tax effects of the different types of investment you may be considering. They can also help you with the preparation of tax returns. Many accountants can also help with raising finance and offer support with the preparation of business plans. Additionally, they may be able to advise in a general way about pensions and your proposed investment strategy.

If you need help in locating a suitable accountant, any of the following should be able to advise:

Association of Chartered Certified Accountants. Enquiries: Tel: 020 7059 5000; email: info@accaglobal.com; website: www.accaglobal.com.

Institute of Chartered Accountants in England and Wales. If your enquiry is regarding membership, a specific member of the ICAEW, or to check if a firm is registered with the ICAEW, please call the ICAEW membership enquiry line on: Tel: 0906 614 0906; or email:members.registration@icaew. co.uk. Please note that if you require confirmation of an ICAEW member in writing, a charge of £20 plus VAT will be levied. For this service please email the details to members.registration@icaew.co.uk; website: www.icaew-firms.co.uk.

Institute of Chartered Accountants of Scotland. Enquiries regarding members registration, call: Tel: 0131 347 0313; email: centralservices@icas.org.uk; website:www.icas.org. uk.

Complaints. Anyone with a complaint against an accountancy firm can contact the Professional Conduct Department of the ICAEW (www.icaew.com).

Banks

Most people need no introduction to the clearing banks, but not all bank customers realise what a comprehensive service their bank provides. In addition to the normal account facilities, all the major high street banks offer investment, insurance and tax-planning services, as well as how to draw up a will. Brief information follows on the main clearing banks but there also are other, more specialised banks such as Hoares and Coutts and overseas banks that are all part of the UK clearing system and can offer a very good service. The addresses given are those of the head office.

Abbey National Plc, 2 Triton Square, Regent's Place, London NW1 3AN. Abbey offers a range of savings, mortgage, pension, current account, medical and other insurance products plus loans for such items as home improvements, a car or money to finance a holiday. A broad range of savings accounts are available that include branch-based, postal and internet instant access accounts; also fixed- and variable-rate savings bonds, including a retirement income bond for the over 55s. There is also a range of ISAs. Full details of all Abbey services can be obtained from any high street branch or by calling Abbey direct on: Tel: 0800 555100; website: www.abbey.com.

Barclays Bank Plc, 1 Churchill Place, London E14 5HP. Barclays Bank offers customers a range of accounts to suit a variety of personal savings requirements. Additionally, a number of financial planning services are available through Barclays Bank subsidiary companies. These include personal investment advice, investment management, stockbroking, unit trusts, personal taxation, wills and trusts. You can apply through your local branch of Barclays Bank or call: Tel: 08457 555 555; website: www.barclays.co.uk.

HSBC, 8 Canada Square, London E14 5HQ. HSBC offers a comprehensive choice of financial products ranging from OEICS and ISAs to life assurance, which are selected according to a customer's requirements by a financial planning manager. HSBC Premier IFA offers investment management and estate planning services to clients who prefer to have a local specialist to look after their affairs on a regular basis. Clients would typically have an income over £75,000 or liquid assets of over £100,000. Any HSBC branch can arrange a meeting if you would like to discuss these services, or call: Tel: 08457 404 404; website: www.hsbc.co.uk.

Lloyds TSB Group, 25 Gresham Street, London EC2V 7HN. Lloyds TSB offers a wide range of financial services, including current and savings accounts, home insurance, investment management and also life assurance, through Scottish Widows. As well as the classic account and the Gold Service, which among other facilities includes free travel insurance, there is Private Banking, which is a comprehensive wealth-management service tailored to individual requirements for customers with £250,000 or more of liquid assets. Details of all these services, as well as life assurance and investment products, are available at all Lloyds TSB branches. Tel: 0845 3 000 000; website: www.lloydstsb.com.

NatWest, 135 Bishopsgate, London EC2M 3UR. NatWest financial planning managers can advise on a wide range of banking and financial planning services for retirement, including investment funds and ISAs. To make an appointment, contact your local NatWest branch or call free on: Tel: 0800 200 400; website: www.natwest.com.

Royal Bank of Scotland, 42 St Andrew Square, Edinburgh EH2 2YE. The Royal Bank of Scotland offers a comprehensive range of current accounts and savings products. The Bank's Private Trust and Taxation Department offers free advice on making a will, although the usual legal fees are applicable if you proceed. Royal Scottish Assurance, the Royal Bank of Scotland's life assurance, pensions and investment company, offers a full financial planning service free of charge. Financial planning consultants can also recommend ISAs and unit trusts provided by the Royal Bank of Scotland unit trust managers. Further information is available from any branch of the Bank or: Tel: 0808 100 0808; website: www.rbs.co.uk.

Complaints. If you have a complaint about a banking matter, you must first try to resolve the issue with the bank or building society concerned. If you remain dissatisfied, you can contact the **Financial Ombudsman Service (FOS)** see details on page 99.

Independent financial advisers (IFAs)

IFAs can advise you across the whole spectrum of investment policies and products: endowment policies, personal pensions, life assurance, permanent health insurance, critical illness cover, unit trusts, ISAs and other forms of personal investment such as mortgages. Their job is to help you work out whether the type of policy you have in mind would be most suitable and where, depending on your circumstances and objectives, you could obtain best value for money. In other words, they act as your personal adviser and handle all the arrangements for you.

In order to be able to offer 'best advice', an IFA needs to try to ensure that you would not be at risk of over-committing yourself or taking some other risk that might jeopardise your security. He/she will, therefore, need an understanding of your existing financial circumstances (and future expectations) including, for example, your earnings, employment prospects and any other types of investment you might already have. In turn, you should also ask your adviser a number of questions including – as a first essential – with whom they are regulated. This should normally be the FSA but could be one of a small number of Designated Professional Bodies, which themselves are answerable to the FSA. If you have any doubts, you can check via the FSA's Central Register on: Tel: 0845 606 1234; website: www.fsa.gov.uk.

Your adviser should provide you with two 'key facts' documents entitled *About our Services* and *About the Cost of our Services*, plus a 'suitability letter' explaining all these points, but if for some reason you do not receive these or if there is anything you do not understand, you should not hesitate to ask. Under rules brought in by the FSA, advisers who want to call themselves independent have to offer clients the option of paying by fee. This means, of course, that clients incur an upfront charge.

The following organisations will be pleased to send you names and addresses of local IFAs.

IFA Promotion Ltd claims it has 90 per cent of the registered IFA market. Tel: 0800 085 3250; email: contact@ifap. org.uk; website: www.unbiased.co.uk.

The **Institute of Financial Planning** will help you in your search for a certified financial planner by region, speciality or name. Tel: 0117 945 2470; email: enquiries@financialplanning.org.uk; website: www.financialplanning.org. uk.

The **Personal Finance Society** (**PFS**) will also help you identify an adviser by postcode or specific financial need. Its website has a useful extra function in that it allows you to look for only chartered financial advisors. Once you have found an adviser, you can make sure that they are approved by checking their credentials with the FSA, who are responsible for regulating the industry. Tel: 020 8530 0852; email: customer.serv@thepfs.org; website: www.thepfs.org.

Insurance brokers

The insurance business covers a very wide range from straightforward policies – such as motor or household insurance – to the rather more complex areas, including life assurance and pensions.

Although many people think of brokers and independent financial advisers (IFAs) as doing much the same job, IFAs specialise in advising on products and policies with some investment content, whereas brokers primarily deal with the more straightforward type of insurance. Some brokers are also authorised to give investment advice. A broker should be able to help you choose the policies that are best suited to you, help you determine how much cover you require and explain any technical terms contained in the documents. He/she can also assist with any claims, remind you when renewals are necessary and advise you on keeping your cover up to date. An essential point to check before proceeding is that the firm the broker represents is regulated by the FSA.

A condition of registration is that a broker must deal with a multiplicity of insurers and therefore be in a position to offer a comprehensive choice of policies. The FSA disclosure rules require brokers to provide potential customers with a 'key facts' document. This should include the cost of the policy (but not commission), as well as a 'suitability' statement explaining the reasons for their recommendation. The information must also draw attention to any significant or unusual exemptions. Generally speaking, you are safer to use a larger brokerage with an established reputation. Also, before you take out a policy, it is advisable to consult several brokers in order to get a better feel for the market. **The British Insurance Brokers' Association** represents nearly 2,200 insurance broking businesses. They can put you in touch with a member broker in your area, contact: Tel: 0870 950 1790; email: enquiries@biba.org.uk; website: www.biba.org.uk.

Complaints

The **Association of British Insurers (ABI)** represents some 400 companies (as opposed to Lloyd's syndicates or brokers), providing all types of insurance from life assurance and pensions to household, motor and other forms of general insurance. About 90 per cent of the worldwide business done by British insurance companies is handled by members of ABI. The ABI publishes a wide range of information sheets, obtainable from the **Association of British Insurers:** Tel: 020 7600 3333; email: info@abi.org.uk; website: www.abi.org.uk.

Other pension advisers

If you have a query to do with your pension, there are some organisations that may be able to assist.

Individuals in paid employment

If you are (or have been) in salaried employment and are a member of an occupational pension scheme, the normal person to ask is your company's personnel manager or pensions adviser – or via them, the pension fund trustees. Alternatively, if you have a problem with your pension you could approach your trade union, since this is an area where most unions are particularly active and well informed.

If you are in need of specific help, a source to try could be the **Pensions Advisory Service**. It has a network of 500 professional advisers who can give free help and advice on all matters to do with any type of pension scheme. There is a local call-rate helpline: Tel: 0845 601 2923; email: enquiries@pensionsadvisoryservice.org.uk; website: www. pensionsadvisoryservice.org.uk.

As with most other financial sectors, there is also a Pensions Ombudsman. You would normally approach the Ombudsman if neither the pension scheme trustees nor the Pensions Advisory Service were able to solve your problem. Also, as with all Ombudsmen, he can only investigate matters that come within his orbit. These are: 1) complaints of maladministration by the trustees, managers or administrators of a pension scheme or by an employer; and 2) disputes of fact or law with the trustees, managers or an employer.

You can write or call direct to **The Pensions Ombudsman**: Tel: 020 7834 9144; email: enquiries@pensionsombudsman. org.uk; website: www.pensions-ombudsman.org.uk.

Unlike many of the other Ombudsman services, the Pensions Ombudsman has not become part of the single statutory Financial Ombudsman Service and will continue to remain as a separate scheme.

Another source of help is the Pension Tracing Service, which can provide individuals with contact details for a pension scheme with which they have lost touch. There is no charge for the service. For further information, contact the **Pension Tracing Service**: Tel: 0845 6002 537. You can also fill out a tracing request form online by visiting the website: www.the pensionservice.gov.uk and following the links to the Pension Tracing Service.

Two other organisations that, although they do not advise on individual cases, are interested in matters of principle and broader issues affecting pensions, are:

National Association of Pension Funds. Tel: 020 7808 1300; email: napf@napf.co.uk; website: www.napf.co.uk.

The Pensions Regulator. Tel: 0870 606 3636; email: customer support@thepensionsregulator.gov.uk; website: www.thepen sionsregulator.gov.uk.

Solicitors

Solicitors are professional advisers on subjects to do with the law or on matters that could have legal implications. They can assist with the purchase or rental of property, with drawing up a will, or if you are charged with a criminal offence or are sued in a civil matter. Additionally, their advice can be invaluable in vetting any important document before you sign it. If you do not have a solicitor, often the best way of finding one is through the recommendation of a friend or other professional adviser, such as an accountant. Another solution would be to contact the Law Society: Tel: 020 7242 1222; email: contact@lawsociety.org.uk; website: www.lawsociety.org.uk.

A further resource of possible interest is **SIFA (Solicitors for Independent Financial Advice)**. This is a network of law firms offering financial as well as legal services, with the aim of providing clients with a 'one-stop shop' when making important financial decisions. It maintains a nationwide register and will send enquirers details of up to six local firms according to whether the type of help needed is to do with investments, pension planning, wills or choosing a long-term care policy. For further information, contact SIFA: Tel: 01372 721172; email: sifa@sifa.co.uk; website: www. sifa.co.uk.

Community Legal Service (Legal Aid) Funding

If you need a Community Legal Service (CLS) solicitor, or want to find out if you are eligible for legal aid, the place to go is a solicitor's office or an advice centre. Ask for leaflet *A Practical Guide to Community Legal Service Funding by the Legal Services Commission*. You can ask an adviser to go through this with you to help you work out whether you are eligible. If you have a low income or are in receipt of benefits and would welcome independent advice about tax credits, debt, employment or housing problems, you might usefully contact the Community Legal Advice Helpline. As well as providing free information, help and advice, the Service lists solicitors and advice agencies that do CLS work: Tel: 0845 345 4345; website: www.legalservices.gov.uk.

Complaints

All solicitors are required by the Law Society to have their own in-house complaints procedure. If you are unhappy about the service you have received, you should first try to resolve the matter with the firm through their complaints-handling partner. If you still feel aggrieved you can approach the Law Society's Legal Complaints Service (LCS), which is an independent arm of the Law Society responsible for handling complaints against solicitors.

If you believe you have a complaint of negligence, the LCS will help you either by putting you in touch with a solicitor specialising in negligence claims or by referring you to the solicitor's insurers. If it arranges an appointment for you with a negligence panelist, the panel solicitor will see you free of charge for up to an hour and advise you as to your best course of action. If you believe that you have been over-charged, you should ask to be sent the booklet *Can We Help?* This explains the procedure for getting your bill checked, the various time limits involved and the circumstances in which you might be successful in getting the fee reduced.

For practical assistance if you are having problems with your solicitor, you can ring the **Legal Complaints Service**

Helpline on: Tel: 0845 608 6565; email: enquiries@legal-complaints.org.uk; website: www.legalcomplaints.org.uk.

If this has failed to resolve the problem, you can approach the Legal Services Ombudsman. You must try to do so within three months of the LCS's, or other professional body's, final decision or your complaint will risk being out of time and the Ombudsman will not be able to help you. Contact the **Legal Services Ombudsman** on: Tel: 0845 601 0794; email: lso@olso.gsi.gov.uk; website: www.olso.org.

General queries. For queries of a more general nature, you should approach **The Law Society**: Tel: 020 7242 1222; email: contact@lawsociety.org.uk; website:www.lawsociety.org.uk.

For those in Scotland and Northern Ireland. If you live in Scotland or Northern Ireland, the LCS will not be able to help you. Instead you should contact the Law Society at the relevant address, as follows:

The Law Society of Scotland. Tel: 0131 226 7411; email: lawscot@lawscot.org.uk; website: www.lawscot.org.uk.

The Law Society of Northern Ireland. Tel: 028 9023 1614; email: info@lawsoc-ni.org; website: www.lawsoc-ni.org.

Stockbrokers

Stockbrokers buy and sell shares quoted on the main market of the London Stock Exchange and on AIM, which trades mainly in the shares of young and growing companies.

Investments can be made in UK and international equities, bonds, investment trusts and gilts (government stocks). As well as trading for clients, stockbrokers can advise on the prospects of different companies; help individuals choose the best type of investment according to their financial situation; and can also provide a wide range of other financial services including tax planning.

It is difficult to be very specific about the cost of using a stockbroker. Although some now charge fees in the same way as, say, a solicitor, generally stockbrokers make their living by charging commission on every transaction. You will need to enquire what the terms and conditions are before committing yourself, as these can vary quite considerably between one firm and another. A growing number of provincial stockbrokers are happy to deal for private investors with sums from about £5,000. Additionally, nearly all major stockbrokers now run unit trusts, because through these they are investing collectively for their clients, they welcome quite modest investors with around £2,000.

There are several ways of finding a stockbroker: you can approach an individual through recommendation; you can check the **London Stock Exchange** website (www.londonstockexchange.com) for its 'Locate a Broker' service. Alternatively there is the **Association of Private Client Investment Managers and Stockbrokers (APCIMS)**, which provides a free directory of stockbrokers and investment managers, together with details of their services. APCIMS also has an online directory, which is searchable by region and type of service: Tel: 020 7247 7080; email: info@ apcims.co.uk; website: www.apcims.co.uk.

Complaints

If you have a complaint about a stockbroker or other member of the former Securities and Futures Authority (SFA), you should put this in writing to the compliance officer of the stockbroking firm involved. If the matter is not satisfactorily resolved, you can then contact the Financial Ombudsman Service (FOS), which will investigate your complaint and, if the Ombudsman considers this justified, can award compensation.

A note of warning. Despite the safeguards of the Financial Services Act, when it comes to investment – or to financial advisers – there are no cast iron guarantees. Under the investor protection legislation, all practitioners and/or businesses they represent offering investment or similar services must be authorised by the FSA or, in certain cases, by a small number of Designated Professional Bodies who themselves are answerable to the FSA. A basic question, therefore, to ask anyone offering investment advice or products is: are you registered and if so by whom? The information is easy to check by telephoning the FSA's Central Register on: Tel: 0845 606 1234; or the FSA website: www.fsa.gov.uk.

Financial Ombudsman Service (FOS)

There is now a single contact point for dissatisfied customers as the FOS covers complaints across almost the entire range of financial services, including consumer-credit activities (such as store cards, credit cards and hire purchase transactions). The service is free and the FOS is empowered to award compensation of up to £100,000. However, before contacting the FOS, you must first try to resolve your complaint with the organisation concerned. Also, the Ombudsman is powerless to act if legal proceedings have been started. For further information, contact the **Financial Ombudsman Service**: Tel: 0845 080 1800; email: complaint. info@financial-ombudsman.org.uk; website: www.financial-ombudsman.org.uk.

Useful reading

Choosing a Financial Adviser – How keyfacts can help you, obtainable free from the FSA: Tel: 0845 606 1234; website: www.fsa.gov.uk.

4

Wills

This book would not be complete without mentioning wills. No one is immortal and anyone who is married, has children or is over the age of 35 should make a will. At the very least, should anything happen, this will ensure that their wishes are known and properly executed. But also, and this is most important, it will spare their family the legal complications that arise when someone dies intestate. A major problem, if someone dies without leaving a will, is that the surviving husband or wife will usually have to wait very much longer for badly needed cash. The legal formalities are infinitely more complex. There will be no executor. Also, the individual's assets will be distributed according to a rigid formula, which may be a far cry from what he/she had intended, and may perversely result in the partner's security being quite unnecessarily jeopardised.

Laws of intestacy

The rules, if you die without leaving a will, are as follows:

▦ If there is **a surviving spouse but no surviving children, parents, brothers, sisters or direct nephews or nieces** of the deceased, the widow/widower inherits the whole of the estate.

▦ If there are **children but no surviving spouse,** the estate is divided equally among the children. If one child has died, his/her share would go to his/her own children.

▦ If there is a **spouse and children,** the partner receives all personal possessions, £125,000 and a life interest in half of the remainder. The other half goes to the children.

▦ If there is a **spouse, no children,** but other close members of the family still living (parents, brothers, sisters, direct nephews or nieces), the surviving spouse receives all personal possessions, £200,000 and half of the remainder of the estate. The other half is divided between the rest of the family.

▦ **Non-married partners** do not inherit automatically; they have to make a court application.

▦ **Same-sex partners** who have entered into a civil partnership have the same inheritance rights as married spouses.

▦ If a **couple are separated,** but not divorced, they are still legally married and, therefore, the separated partner could be a major beneficiary.

Making a will

You have three choices: you can do it yourself, you can ask your bank to help you, or you can use a solicitor or a specialist will-writing practitioner.

Doing it yourself

Home-made wills are not generally recommended. People often use ambiguous wording, which, although perfectly clear to the individual who has written it, may be less than obvious to others. This could result in the donor's wishes being misinterpreted and could also cause considerable delay in settling the estate.

You can buy forms from WH Smith and other stationers that, although helpful, are not perfect and still leave considerable margin for error. For individuals with sight problems, RNIB has produced a comprehensive guide to making or changing a will, which is available in large print size, Braille and on tape, as well as in standard print size. This is obtainable free by contacting the Donor Development department at **RNIB**: Tel: 08457 66 99 99; website: www.rnib.org.uk.

Two witnesses are needed and an essential point to remember is that beneficiaries cannot witness a will; nor can the spouses of any beneficiaries. In certain circumstances, a will can be rendered invalid. A sensible precaution for anyone doing it themselves is to have it checked by a solicitor or by a legal expert from the Citizens Advice Bureau.

Banks

Advice on wills and the administration of estates is carried out by the trustee companies of most of the major high street banks. In particular, the services they offer are to provide general guidance, to act as executor and to administer the estate. They will also introduce clients to a solicitor and keep a copy of the will – plus other important documents – in their safe, to avoid the risk of their being mislaid. Additionally, banks (as solicitors) can give tax planning and other financial guidance, including advice on inheritance tax. Some banks will draw up a will for you.

Solicitors

Solicitors may offer to draw up a will, act as executors and administer the estate. Like banks, they will also of course keep a copy of your will in safe-keeping (most will not charge for storing a will). If you do not have a solicitor, you can contact the Law Society: Tel: 020 7242 1222; email: contact@lawsociety.org.uk; website: www.lawsociety.org.uk.

Alternatively, if you simply want help in writing a will, you could consult a specialist will-writing practitioner. The best approach is to contact one of the following organisations:

The Society of Will Writers will be pleased to send you an information pack together with details of up to three of their members in your area. Contact: Tel: 01522 687888; website: www.thesocietyofwillwriters.co.uk.

The Will Bureau writes wills, offers estate-planning advice and once it has written your will, regularly updates you with developments in the law that could affect your estate and inheritance tax. For further information, contact: Tel: 020 8920 3360; email: info@twb.org.uk; website: www.twb. org.uk.

Another company that could help you prepare a will is **Trust Inheritance Limited**. It provides a home-visit will-writing service and all work is professionally drafted by a solicitor-led team. For further information, contact: Tel: 08000 97 80 12; website: www.trustinheritance.com.

Charges

These can vary enormously, depending on the size and complexity of the will. A basic will could cost around £120, or, if your affairs are more complicated, the cost could reach hundreds of pounds. Always ask for an estimate before proceeding. Remember too that professional fees normally carry VAT. Some solicitors charge according to the time they spend on a job, so don't spend hours discussing your will, or changing it every few months. Most solicitors will give you a fixed-fee estimate for a will, so you should have a good idea from the outset what it would cost. The fees for will-writing practitioners are broadly in line with those of solicitors, starting from about £60.

Community Legal Service Funding – legal aid

Financial assistance for legal help and advice is available to certain groups of people for making a will. These include:

people aged over 70; disabled people; and a parent of a disabled person whom they wish to provide for in their will. Additionally, to qualify, they will need to satisfy the financial eligibility criteria. For further information enquire at your Citizens Advice Bureau or other advice centre.

Executors

You will need to appoint at least one executor to administer your will. An executor can be a beneficiary under the estate and can be a member of your family or a friend whom you trust to act impartially, always provided of course that he/she is willing to accept the responsibility. You could appoint your solicitor or bank; their fees will be additional. They are not paid at the time of making the will but instead the fees come out of the estate. Pretty significant sums could be involved, the only way to discover is to get an estimate from each.

Banks publish a tariff of their charges. Solicitors render bills according to the time involved, so, although it is impossible for them to be precise, they should nevertheless be able to give a pretty accurate assessment. Both banks' and solicitors' fees may increase during the interval between their being appointed and fulfilling their duties as executor.

Other points

Wills should always be kept in a safe place – and their

whereabouts known. The most sensible arrangement is for the solicitor to keep the original and for both you and the bank to have a copy.

A helpful initiative devised by the Law Society is a mini-form, known as a **Personal Assets Log**. This is for individuals drawing up a will to give to their executor or close relatives. It is, quite simply, a four-sided leaflet with space to record the essential information: name and address of solicitor; where the will and other important documents – for example, share certificates and insurance policies – are kept; the date of any codicils; and so on. Logs should be obtainable from most solicitors.

Wills may need updating in the event of an important change of circumstances, for example a divorce, remarriage or the birth of a grandchild. An existing will normally becomes invalid in the event of marriage or remarriage and should be replaced. Any changes must be by codicil (for minor alterations) or by a new will, and must be properly witnessed.

Another reason why you may need, or wish, to change your will is in consequence of the new inheritance-tax rules affecting accumulation and maintenance trusts, as well as interest-in-possession trusts. The Law Society had been advising all owners of homes/other assets worth more than the nil-rate band (£312,000 for the 2008/09 tax year) to review their will, if any of their assets have been left in trust.

Partners who wish to leave all their possessions to each other should consider including 'a survivorship clause' in their wills, as an insurance against the intestacy rules being applied were they both to be involved in the same fatal accident. Legal advice is strongly recommended here.

Finally, **Help the Aged** has a team of locally based wills and legacy advisers who provide confidential, impartial advice to older people in their own homes about all aspects of making, or revising, a will. The advice service is available free of charge to anyone of retirement age.

Useful reading

Making Your Will. Free factsheet from **Age Concern**: Tel: 0800 009966; website: www.AgeConcern.org.uk. A separate Scottish version is available.

Will Information Pack. Free from Wills and Legacies Department, **Help the Aged**: Tel: 020 7278 1114; website: www.helptheaged.org.uk.

Stop press

VAT

A 2.5 per cent cut in VAT (from 17.5 per cent to 15 per cent) took effect from 1 December 2008. But this is only for 13 months, until the end of 2009, after which time it will return to the original rate. VAT is not charged on some goods, such as food and children's clothing, so there are no savings in these areas.

This reduction is offset by increased duties on alcohol, tobacco and petrol. Also there is no benefit for gas and electricity customers since VAT is already charged at a lower rate of 5 per cent, which has not changed.

Personal tax

The increase in the personal allowance to offset the scrapping of the 10p tax band has been made permanent and increased to £145 per year in April 2009 from £120. This should benefit 22 million basic-rate taxpayers.

Allowances

In April 2009, the amount of income that is free of tax will increase from £6,035 to £6,475 for single people up to the age of 65 – an increase of £440.

For those over 65 up to 74 years, the increase will be from £9,030 (2008/09) to £9,490 (2009/10) – up £460.

For those over 75, the increase is from £9,180 (2008/09) to £9,640 (2009/10) – an increase of £460.

Personal allowances will be scrapped for those earning in excess of £140,000 a year from April 2010.

Income tax

From 2011 income tax will be charged at 45 per cent on all earnings about £150,000. This will affect the top 1 per cent of earners.

Inheritance tax threshold

No change.

Summary

Working on the premise that it is better to be an owl than an ostrich, this book focuses on making the best of what you've got. The first part related to tax: what you could be paying and what steps you can take to ensure you are not paying too much, and where savings can be made. The second part covered what sort of investments are available and discussed ways of assessing what is right for you and where to get appropriate advice. The third section covered financial advisers; who regulates them; and how to check that you are getting best advice. Also, if appropriate, where you can apply for help if you have a complaint or you think something has gone wrong. The final section dealt with Wills and other important related matters. With this information you should feel more confident about making the most of your money so that you can enjoy future years in comfort and prosperity.

Notes

ALSO AVAILABLE FROM KOGAN PAGE

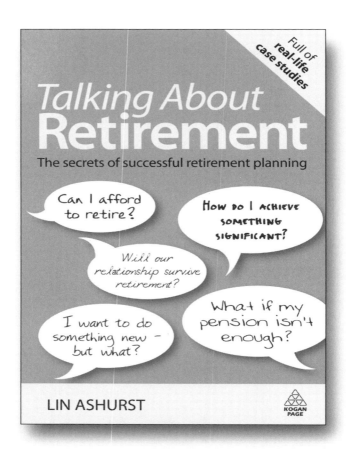

ISBN: 978 0 7494 5515 6   Paperback   2009

Order online now at www.koganpage.com

Sign up for regular e-mail updates on new
Kogan Page books in your interest area

ALSO AVAILABLE FROM KOGAN PAGE

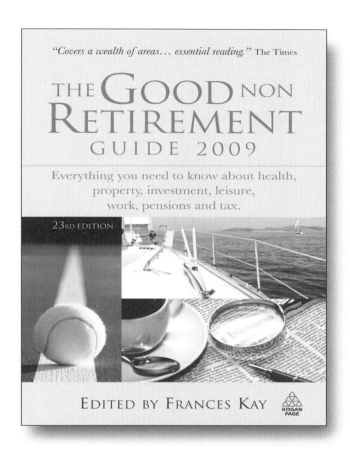

ISBN: 978 0 7494 5272 8   Paperback   2009

Order online now at www.koganpage.com

Sign up for regular e-mail updates on new
Kogan Page books in your interest area

The sharpest minds need the finest advice

visit
www.koganpage.com
today

You're reading one of the thousands of books published by Kogan Page, Europe's largest independent business publisher. We publish a range of books and electronic products covering business, management, marketing, logistics, HR, careers and education. Visit our website today and sharpen your mind with some of the world's finest thinking.